NATIONWIDE F
THRIVING AND SURVIVING ON CAMPUS . . .

Rowman & Littlefield is pleased to publish *Thriving and Surviving on Campus,* the Third Edition of *An Insider's Guide to Community College Administration.*

First published in 2000, *Insider's Guide* quickly rose to the bestseller list on the American Association of Community College's website bookstore as college administrators, university graduate students, and staff development officers recognized the importance of the book as a learning and mentoring resource for current and future community college staff.

> One community college administrator association called it "a nitty-gritty leadership guide," encouraging its members to use the book as a personal and professional handbook.
>
> The *Community College Journal of Research and Practice* described it as "rich in advice and wise insights predicated on experience."
>
> The *University Business* magazine book reviewer proclaimed, "Small can be beautiful. The authors have laid out one of the shrewdest and most candid guides for anyone hoping to be a dean or president."
>
> The book has been particularly popular among faculty teaching in university, college, and community college administrative development programs, including Stanford University School of Education, the University of Florida Institute of Higher Education, the Association of California Community College Administrators 101 Summer Seminar, the University of Houston community colleges seminar course, Old Dominion University's Community College Leadership & Program Development, the Asilomar (Monterey, California) Leadership Skills Seminar, and the Roueche Graduate Center, National American University.

Thriving and Surviving on Campus represents an updating of the bestselling first and second editions of *An Insider's Guide.* The authors have addressed new issues on the community college administrative scene as well as identified new challenges—and solutions—on the horizon.

Rowman & Littlefield is proud to offer this new edition to our readers.

The Editors

Thriving and Surviving on Campus

An Insider's Guide to Community College Administration

Third Edition

Robert Jensen
Ray Giles

ROWMAN & LITTLEFIELD
Lanham • Boulder • New York • London

Published by Rowman & Littlefield
An imprint of The Rowman & Littlefield Publishing Group, Inc.
4501 Forbes Boulevard, Suite 200, Lanham, Maryland 20706
www.rowman.com

86-90 Paul Street, London EC2A 4NE, United Kingdom

British Library Cataloguing in Publication Information Available

Library of Congress Cataloging-in-Publication Data

Names: Jensen, Robert, 1940– author. | Giles, Ray, author.
Title: Thriving and surviving on campus : an insider's guide to community
  college administration / Robert Jensen, Ray Giles.
Description: Third edition. | Lanham, Maryland : Rowman & Littlefield,
  2024. | Revised edition of: Insider's guide to community college
  administration. 2nd ed. Washington, DC : American Association of
  Community Colleges, ©2006. | Summary: "The book offers a real-world
  perspective of the inner workings of community colleges in the third
  edition of this popular book. The stories and scenarios the authors
  share paint a realistic picture of the complex landscape of community
  college organizational structures, leadership, and governance. The
  advice they offer is practical and based upon their vast experience in
  positions of college leadership. If you are interested in learning more
  about community colleges, how expectations change when moving into a
  leadership position, how to move up in leadership, and how to avoid
  institutional landmines, you will find this book to be a valuable
  resource"— Provided by publisher.
Identifiers: LCCN 2023029480 (print) | LCCN 2023029481 (ebook) | ISBN
  9781475873436 (cloth) | ISBN 9781475873443 (paperback) | ISBN
  9781475873450 (epub)
Subjects: LCSH: Community colleges—United States—Administration.
Classification: LCC LB2341 .J53 2024 (print) | LCC LB2341 (ebook) | DDC
  378.1/010973—dc23/eng/20230714
LC record available at https://lccn.loc.gov/2023029480
LC ebook record available at https://lccn.loc.gov/2023029481

To our friends, colleagues, and mentors who have taught us, tolerated us,
and helped make our careers meaningful and enjoyable,
and to Earl L. Klapstein, community college president and chancellor

Contents

Foreword

Thriving and Surviving on Campus

Robert Jensen and Ray Giles offer a real-world perspective of the inner workings of community colleges in the third edition of their popular book, *Thriving and Surviving on Campus: An Insider's Guide to Community College Administration.* The stories and scenarios they share paint a realistic picture of the complex landscape of community college organizational structures, leadership, and governance. The advice they offer is practical and based upon their vast experience in positions of college leadership.

If you are interested in learning more about community colleges, how expectations change when moving into a leadership position, how to move up in leadership, and how to avoid institutional landmines, you will find this book to be a valuable resource. Topics include institutional politics, the importance of personal and professional "fit" when considering a new position, paying attention to what is most important, risk-taking, managing institutional change, commuter marriages, using consultants effectively, leading in a climate of shared governance, negotiating CEO employment contracts, board and CEO relations, surviving votes of no confidence, and knowing when it is time to leave a CEO position.

The authors also provide insight on the role of trustees and effective college governance. Topics include motivation for becoming a trustee, governance responsibilities, communication, conflicts of interest, and CEO selection and evaluation. The governance chapter is valuable for trustees, those who are considering running for the board or seeking an appointment, and others who just want to know more about effective college governance.

Thriving and Surviving on Campus is an important contribution to the understanding of community colleges and the people who make them work. The book should be read and kept handy by those who are serious about community college leadership and governance.

George R. Boggs, PhD
President and CEO Emeritus, American Association of Community Colleges
Superintendent/President Emeritus, Palomar College
Chair, Phi Theta Kappa Board of Directors

Preface

Every profession has its written and unwritten rules about how to be successful. Community college leadership is no exception. This book is about how to survive, thrive, and make a difference as a community college leader in the political arena that can sometimes be overwhelming. We will share ideas, anecdotes, and vicarious experiences that should help you take advantage of career opportunities and, if necessary, survive any pitfalls that may temporarily set you back.

For example, years ago we knew a community college chancellor who had built a national reputation for educational innovation and service to students. At the peak of his popularity and esteem, his business manager walked into his office one day and announced that the college district was on the edge of fiscal collapse. The business manager had made a series of bad guesses and had been afraid to notify his famous and often out-of-town boss. Now, like a championship skier at the bottom of a hill looking up at an oncoming avalanche, the well-respected college leader stood defenseless as the board, the faculty, and the community overwhelmed him, first demanding answers and ultimately his resignation.

All of us make mistakes sometime during our careers. Whether you're a college administrator, faculty leader, college trustee, or have made it to the top as a college president or chancellor, this book can widen your perspective and perhaps help you avoid getting blindsided like our friend in the story.

For college administrators, the story illustrates a theme we will touch on throughout the book: *You can be a well-respected leader, be in demand as a conference speaker, and have people calling you for advice, but you better keep an eye on your own shop if you want to keep your reputation intact.* This book will help you focus on the important issues and give you some helpful ideas on how to handle those issues in the best interest of students, your institution, and your career.

For faculty leaders and others who want to be administrators, this book will give you insights into community college leadership and how the challenges of college leadership intermingle with faculty politics. We will also help answer a basic question for many readers: Should I take the plunge into college administration?

For university graduate students, the book is a valuable resource as you think about your future personal and career goals. Much of what we talk about, including the rewards and the downsides of administrative leadership, are usually available only via on-the-job training. We have attempted here to provide a candid and realistic overview of the issues, challenges, and pitfalls of life as an administrator.

College trustees can benefit from our inside-the-campus look at the challenges facing today's community college administrators and from our experience on how trustees can best serve their institutions and provide dynamic leadership.

Likewise, community college administrators may find our insights on the role of and challenges faced by community college trustees helpful as they move forward in their role as campus leaders.

We have held just about every job in the classroom and the executive suite, from teaching and faculty leadership roles to campus dean, vice president, president, and chancellor. During our careers, we worked in nine community college districts—from a small single-college to large multicollege and multicampus college districts—in three states. We have not only driven the bus, we have worked under the hood, changed the tires, and have the dirty fingernails and bruises to prove it. Let us help you learn from our mistakes, missteps, and successes.

—Robert Jensen and Ray Giles

Introduction

The "Ten Truths of Community College Leadership" found at the end of this book is both the foundation for and a summation of the entire book.

If the reader is so inclined, start by reading the "Ten Truths" for a quick preview of the issues, information, and insights addressed in *Thriving and Surviving on Campus*. (And the authors promise that after reading chapters 1 through 5, you will have an even clearer and more nuanced understanding of the "Ten Truths" and how they can apply to your career.)

Chapters 1 through 4 are linear in terms of the transition and maturation of an administrator's career. Chapter 5 is a stand-alone, in that it provides information on how boards and trustees should—but sometimes don't—interact with the CEO and her staff, the faculty, and the community.

Chapter 1, "What Am I Getting Into? Choices and Personal Decisions," provides an overview of the campus turf, what it means to be an administrator in different types of college districts, and some of the choices to be made in your career.

Chapter 2, "Thriving and Surviving on the Job," addresses what administrators do on the macrolevel and the skills needed to succeed.

Chapter 3, "Institutional Politics," is just that. Community college administration is a contact sport and here we address some of the internal issues you're guaranteed to face on any campus in any state at any level.

Chapter 4, "Presidential Issues," is not only for those planning to become CEOs, but is relevant to every member of a college staff since most interact to one degree or another with the president or chancellor and all are certain to be affected by his decisions.

And because trustees are legally empowered to establish college policy and—most important—to hire and fire the CEO, chapter 5, "Not for Trustees

Only," provides insights on the interaction between boards and their CEO, a matter of importance to most community college administrators.

Finally, "Ten Truths of Community College Leadership" are concepts, rules, and warnings applicable to every administrator on a college campus and, we hope, directly helpful to you in your career.

Terminology Used in This Book

Titles and job descriptions commonly used in community colleges can be misleading. For example, the title of college president may represent someone who runs one college or several. He or she may also be called a chancellor or chief executive officer (CEO). To minimize this confusion, we will use the following designations:

Single-college district: a college district with one main campus that can include off-campus centers and other sites but with a single accreditation.

Multicollege district: multiple colleges that are independently accredited and administered by college presidents who report to a district chancellor.

Multicampus college district: multiple campuses administered by a district chancellor/president with campus sites administered by presidents/ directors or other titles. The district is accredited as one college.

Board of trustees: elected or appointed citizens who serve as the governing board of a community college or college district.

CEO: the chief executive officer of a community college district, whether a single-college district, or a multicollege or multicampus college district. We use the term in place of chancellor or president.

Chancellor: the CEO of a multicollege district or multicampus college district.

President: typically, the CEO at a single-college district or a campus in a multicollege district or multicampus college district. At campuses in a multicollege or multicampus district, presidents report to the chancellor.

Vice president or vice chancellor: a second-level administrator found on the campus or in a district office.

Dean: the third level of administration below the vice president but above the program directors, supervisors, and department chairpersons. We use the term to designate a middle-management position. We recognize that at some colleges, the dean is actually a vice president.

Faculty: instructors, counselors, program directors, and librarians serving on the front line of a community college's educational mission.

Management or administrative employees: certified and noncertified employees hired by the board of trustees to oversee the operation of a community college or community college district.

Staff: classified or noncertified employees that play a big—and often unrecognized—part in making a community college function successfully.

1

What Am I Getting Into?

Choices and Personal Decisions

It is not the same to talk of bulls as to be in the bullring.

—Spanish proverb

THE FIRST MANAGEMENT EXPERIENCE

So you want to be a community college administrator. Congratulations. It's a great career choice, full of professional and personal challenges and rewards. But before you turn in that application, let us make a few points.

People who are attracted to administration are sometimes exactly the kind of people who should not be administrators. Some would-be administrators, for example, have erroneous ideas about status and power. The reality is that in many colleges, union and faculty senate leaders have a lot more power and influence than administrators or middle managers and are more apt to be wined and dined by the powers that be. Power and status do not automatically come with an administrative title but, in the community college setting, are more often the result of the painstaking process of building consensus, trust, and confidence.

If you're a powerful faculty leader thinking of becoming an administrator, remember this: As the faculty union or senate leader dealing with the board of trustees, CEO, or college president, you have leverage. You deal with issues of great concern to faculty. You may even have the moral authority to set the faculty agenda or the legal authority to appoint the chief negotiator or grievance chair, or make other decisions. But when you're an administrator, such as a dean, you are in some ways caught between faculty and top administration. You may be held accountable for your decisions but not be given the authority

1

or power to solve problems. As a dean, you have to live with the bureaucratic structure that must be dealt with, adjusted to, and struggled against nearly every day. You also must learn to say the single most horrible and spine-chilling two-letter word in the English language: no. Or you may find yourself wanting to say no for the good of students, but your supervisor, the vice president, or the CEO won't let you. That's life in the administrative ranks.

On the other hand, community college administration can be exciting and rewarding, especially on graduation day when the students and faculty and college community come together to celebrate the accomplishments of the entire institution. (For us, graduation day has always been a highlight of the academic year. You may have had a tough year with your staff, with the faculty, or with the board, but graduation day is a great reminder of why we are in the business.)

Still wondering if you want to be an administrator? Ask yourself the following questions:

- Were you uncomfortable being a department chair, listening to the complaints of your colleagues? That's a warning sign. Don't think about it any further. Instead, stay in the classroom and continue making an important contribution to higher education.
- Are you uncomfortable making no-win decisions, where a significant number of people will disagree with you no matter what side you come down on? If so, don't consider a career in administration.
- Are you a faculty member used to receiving encouragement and support from your supervisor? Ask yourself if you'll feel comfortable switching over to the other side—the side that gives out the pats and holds the hands but is criticized publicly and, sometimes, frequently.
- Ask yourself if you can deal with what we call the turncoat phenomenon. That's when you were drinking coffee at Starbucks with your faculty colleagues one week, and the next week, after being appointed to an administrative position, you're being accused of not knowing what's happening in the classroom. In other words, are you prepared to lose friends by jumping over to the "other team"?

Or is your personality such that you can live with ambiguity and disruption, limited compliments but plenty of unjust criticism and pressure? Can you accept that community colleges operate within the framework of contradictory governance structures: faculty groups that want to make decisions on budget and hiring but reject accountability; boards of trustees, faculty leaders, and administrators battling for turf; and state and federal bureaucracies imposing mandates from afar? Some people just aren't plumbed that way.

But if you want to make a difference for community colleges and students by providing leadership to people, budgets, and programs, read on.

There are numerous ways to find out if administration is right for you. Faculty leadership roles in the senate or the union or chairing the curriculum or budget committee are good starting points. Each of these experiences gives you a feeling for institutional politics and the tug and pull of a campus community—and whether you have the talent and stomach for it. Each of these experiences also tests whether you have the people skills necessary to lead groups and get things done and make people happy doing it. You either have these skills or you don't. They can't be learned in graduate school.

We have a friend who was a powerful faculty leader who also wanted an administrative experience during his career. He waited and picked his spot carefully—a dean's job in an off-campus center. He had overall responsibility for instruction, student services, and administrative services at the off-campus center. The center had its own budget, student government, school newspaper, and graduation ceremony. It was a lot more work than being a division dean but also a lot more fun and rewarding.

But there was a downside to this perfect job. Since the off-campus center was thirty miles from the main campus, the CEO and board of trustees kept a close eye on the center's activities, much more so than any division or department on campus. And what they couldn't see they worried about. As a result, the off-campus dean spent considerable time in meetings on the main campus with top administrators keeping them informed of the instructional, student services, and budget issues as well as local community politics at his off-campus site.

Then the problems really began. A member of the college board of trustees who lived a mile away from the center began to think of it as "his" center. When the dean became popular in the community and began to be quoted extensively in the local press, the trustee (who wasn't quoted in the local press at all) started complaining to the CEO that the center dean was "out of control." The perfect job quickly became a big headache for the new dean as his success and visibility overshadowed the political and ego needs of the trustee.

By the way, if you are a faculty leader, this may or may not surprise you, but it's not a straight-across move from faculty leader to college vice president. Some statewide faculty leaders are even convinced they are ready for a campus presidency. But just because they're comfortable giving speeches to administrative groups, the board of trustees, or state associations doesn't mean they're ready to run a college. It's a completely different job requiring different job skills. Time spent in the lower and middle administration really does matter. There are valuable lessons to be learned working—and struggling—in the administrative ranks.

WHO IS MORE POWERFUL?

We once worked with a board member who made his living as a divorce attorney. He called up a campus dean who was hiring an administrative assistant and instructed the dean to hire a client of his. "She needs a job so she can pay her legal bills," he said. The trustee concluded the conversation by making a not-too-subtle threat to have the dean fired if his orders weren't followed.

What did the dean do? Contact the president? Tell the trustee where to go? No, he called the one person he knew who could handle the situation—the faculty union president. The faculty leader, who had both guts and tenure, called the trustee and threatened to have him disbarred if he ever called the dean on the matter again. End of calls.

THE NEXT STEP: CLIMBING THE ORGANIZATIONAL LADDER

As a program director or assistant dean, your sphere of impact—the degree to which you influence collegewide policy and budgeting—is limited. But as you begin to move up the organization to dean or vice president, your sphere of influence expands dramatically. Suddenly, the programs for which you are responsible have significant day-to-day implications for the entire institution.

If you're thinking of taking this next step in your career, professional and political growth becomes even most critical. Take steps to widen your perspective beyond your expertise and knowledge in order to sharpen your ability to see how programs and decisions affect the institution horizontally and vertically.

By horizontally, we mean the ability to understand and put into context how your programs will fit across the wide spectrum of programs offered by the college and how decisions and actions taken by your program have an impact across the institution. By vertically, we mean the ability to communicate both up and down the chain of command and explain to others—such as your subordinates, as well as your CEO and board of trustees—how your programs are affected by various budget, personnel, political, and education decisions.

A program director focuses on making his or her program meet the college's goals and objectives. But even program directors can't be myopic. They have to understand the ripple effect. For example, if you're in charge of the registration office, you must understand the gravity of the problem created if you lose just one potential student in the registration process to a clerk who rejects the application because the i's weren't dotted or the t's crossed. Over a period of four semesters, rejecting this one student could cost the institution thousands of dollars.

As a dean or vice president managing several programs, you'll need to ensure that your staff understands the interconnectivity of the entire institution. (In this information technology world we live in, this is particularly important.)

One immediate consequence of moving up the administrative ladder is moving from being a tiny blip on everyone's radar to being a giant Boeing 747. Ask yourself—can I take occasional fire, the emotion of no-win decisions, or the pain of justified and unjustified criticism?

If you've been a dean for several years and now want to move up to a vice presidency on campus, here's a fact of campus life you want to keep in mind: there may be an anti-(*your name here*) constituency on campus that would rather bring in a fresh face from off campus for that job you covet so much. The outsider often looks better even if no one has taken a close look.

Unlike the veteran dean who may have had to make a bunch of tough decisions, the perfect stranger hasn't alienated any staff, faculty, or administrators, some of whom may now sit on the selection committee. (For a possible solution, see section "The Nomadic Lifestyle" later in this chapter.)

THE BIG STEP: PRESIDENT AND CEO

Being a college president or CEO is a job for jugglers. You have to be a business manager, fundraiser, chief policy maven, keeper of the academic flame, hand-holder, backslapper, art and athletic devotee, childcare and technology advocate, a pretty good public speaker, and an even better vote counter. The job is complex, fragmented, time-consuming, and physically and emotionally demanding. It's also the best job in the world if you get a kick out of helping an institution do a better job of educating students and serving the community.

The reality is that any style of leadership will work, given the right mix of timing, skill, will, and yes, luck. There are great presidents who have lasted five, ten, twenty years, and there are mediocre presidents who have lasted five, ten, twenty years. There are successful CEOs who believe in top-down management, and there are successful CEOs who believe in bottom-up collaboration.

Taking risks, being thick-skinned, and wanting to be in charge are all part of what makes a president a president. If you're worried about where you'll be five years from now, don't even think of applying for a CEO job. Stay in middle management or go back to the classroom. You'll sleep better and so will your spouse.

How can you know when you're ready for the top job? There are a couple of signs. One is when you become a leader on campuswide issues or when other colleges or state associations begin to turn to you for advice and leadership. Or when you are put into situations that require you to lead others—and you like it. Another is when you know your experience and ideas can make a positive contribution to an institution and you are willing to suffer the "slings and arrows" to help students and faculty succeed.

As you think about climbing the next rung in the administrative career ladder, it's also valuable to understand that the higher you go up, the tougher it is to come back down without falling on your face and causing yourself a lot of pain and embarrassment. Community colleges, unlike universities, don't usually give the unsuccessful top manager a smooth ride back to the faculty ranks. It's something to think about for your family's financial and mental health.

THE DIFFERENCE BETWEEN BEING PRESIDENT AND BEING CEO

We once attended a board meeting in a large multicollege district where we watched the chancellor, sitting casually at the board table, gesture to one of his campus presidents. A campus president, seated at a table in front of the board, stood up and walked around the back of the board table and leaned down so he could hear the chancellor's words of wisdom. The chancellor swiveled around in his big chair and in a stage-whisper said, "Get me a cup of coffee, would you, Mr. President?"

During a break in the meeting, the campus president left the room seething. In the hallway he ran into the faculty union president, who was grinning from ear to ear. What, the faculty union leader asked the college president, had he learned from that? Before he could answer, the faculty leader said, "I think what you learned is that you are staff and probably have a lot less power than I do: because I would not have gotten his coffee."

There are three types of presidencies in community colleges: the CEO/ president of a single-college district, the chancellor of a multicollege district or multicampus college district, and a campus president in a multicollege district or multicampus college district. These have their similarities and their differences, their upsides and downsides.

CEO/PRESIDENT OF A SINGLE-COLLEGE DISTRICT

CEO jobs in a single-college district are different from CEO jobs in a multicampus college district or multicollege district. The single-college district president has a pretty good finger on the pulse of the college and the community. The CEO has staff right there on campus that can help meet goals. And even if vice presidents oppose an idea, a single-college CEO can still sell a program or idea to the campus by walking the halls and talking with people to build consensus.

CEO/PRESIDENT OF SINGLE-COLLEGE DISTRICT

Advantages

- A constituency (community residents and civic leaders, students and campus employees).
- Less buck passing since there is less bureaucracy.
- You call the shots.
- More visibility and respect in the community.
- Much easier for a president to deal with districtwide politics and relationships than a multicollege or multicampus chancellor.

Disadvantages

- No peers to confer with (unlike in a multicollege district).
- Nowhere to hide, nowhere to run.
- As the big fish in a smaller pond, you have more accountability and visibility.
- A lot of care and feeding of the board.

CHANCELLOR OF A MULTICOLLEGE OR MULTICAMPUS COLLEGE DISTRICT

On the other hand, if you're chancellor of a multicollege district or multicampus college district, the only halls you may walk are at the district office, which, of course, is no place to build consensus. A chancellor of a multicollege district doesn't have the intimacy with faculty, staff, and students that campus presidents enjoy. And, unlike campus presidents, the chancellor has no real constituency outside the board of trustees and district office bureaucracy. That's why many multicampus college district CEOs try to build a communitywide sense of the college through public relations. One common strategy is to form a districtwide foundation or advisory committee to bring in civic and business leaders who can sometimes help a district increase its visibility and build a constituency in the community.

Moving an agenda is tougher in multicollege or multicampus college districts. As chancellor you may find it is more difficult to change a big, complex district's culture or climate or initiate districtwide initiatives. Accreditation issues alone can gum up districtwide initiatives in multicollege districts.

In fact, the chancellor's success in moving an agenda depends not only on his or her vision and persuasiveness but on the degree of independence and autonomy of the campuses and the loyalty, support, and effectiveness of the presidents. If the presidents are team players, the chancellor's vision can be implemented with hard work, money, and/or time. If the campuses, on the other hand, operate as independent satellites, rotating in their own orbits, the chancellor can spend a lot of time and effort treading water.

CHANCELLOR OF A MULTICOLLEGE DISTRICT

Advantages

- The ability to initiate districtwide change for students and the community via initiatives and campus climate change.
- Fewer on-campus hassles (you don't have to worry about whether the classrooms are clean).
- Fewer on-campus activities, such as plays and sporting events to attend.
- Usually fewer campus-related town-and-gown activities to attend.
- You're dealing with fewer day-to-day micro-operational issues.
- Higher salary and better benefits.
- More opportunities for state and national visibility.

Disadvantages

- No constituency (and limited interaction with students and faculty).
- Difficult to move an agenda without buy-in and support of college presidents.
- Less visibility in the community.
- More demand from some trustees for care and feeding.
- Scapegoat for college campus issues that are either mishandled or passed up to the district office.
- Need to coordinate and track community outreach by campus presidents to avoid conflict and unnecessary or unwelcomed competition among presidents for students and resources.

CHANCELLOR OF A MULTICAMPUS COLLEGE DISTRICT

Advantages

- Better opportunities to initiate districtwide change for students and the community in initiatives and campus climate change than at a multicollege district.
- Fewer on-campus hassles than faced by a single-college district CEO.
- Fewer on-campus activities such as plays and sporting events to attend than a single-college district CEO but more than a chancellor of a multicollege district.
- Increased town-and-gown activities and greater opportunity to increase visibility for the district in the community.
- Higher salary and better benefits.

Disadvantages

- Nowhere to hide, nowhere to run.
- No peers, such as college presidents, in your district to consult with.
- Intense care and feeding of the board.
- Greater demand for care and feeding of the community. You don't have a college president to send in your place. You're it.
- More accountability. The buck stops at your desk more often, much like a single-college district CEO. You can't blame a campus president.
- The chancellor/president needs to be more involved in both the micro-operational issues as well as the macro-operational issues of the district than does a multicollege district chancellor.

PRESIDENT IN A MULTICAMPUS COLLEGE OR MULTICOLLEGE DISTRICT

Presidents of colleges in multicollege or multicampus college districts have, in many ways, the best jobs in the business. They get to do all the fun things associated with educating students and running a college without the board hassles. They can even, if they choose, pass the tough decisions up the line to their boss, the chancellor.

However, until you work directly for a board, you're still on the second team. Many presidents are comfortable with that role and use their title and their college's mission and reputation to their advantage. We've seen quite a few multicollege district presidents leverage their title and their institution's name for grants, programs, and recognition on a national scale. We've even seen one or two become better known than their boss, the chancellor.

PRESIDENT IN A MULTICAMPUS COLLEGE OR MULTICOLLEGE DISTRICT

Advantages

- A buffer (the chancellor) between you and the board.
- A constituency (faculty, staff, and students).
- Less accountability.
- More job security.
- No collective bargaining responsibility.
- Focus on student learning and student services and meeting the needs of the campus service area.

Disadvantages

- Don't call the shots on the big issues.
- Subject to oversight and meddling from the district office.
- Handle some petty issues from campus faculty, staff, and other administrators.
- Unproductive competition with fellow presidents at districtwide meetings and sometimes in the larger community when college interests overlap across college service areas.
- Lower salary than chancellor.

THE SINGLE-COLLEGE DISTRICT

We once worked at a community college that was the pride and joy of the community. Whenever relatives visited from out-of-state, the family would pack them into the car and drive them over to the college for a look. The college was the educational, cultural, and community center of the town and a place of special pride for its citizenry.

The United States is full of towns where the local community college serves as the centerpiece of the community. Selecting the type of district you want to work in—single-campus, multicollege, small, urban, suburban—is an important part of the career-building process.

For administrators and faculty working at single-college districts, the support of the community can be a many-faceted blessing. All the resources and energies available to the college are focused on the campus. With just one

CEO, his or her responsibilities become clear: provide leadership to the college and maximize the educational opportunities for students.

The same goes for the board of trustees whose time, commitments, and sense of accountability are wrapped up in this single campus. We've found that boards in single-college districts tend to be far more responsive to the community than boards in urban multicollege districts, where campus constituencies are more likely to hold sway and each college must compete aggressively for attention, respect, and budget.

The alumni in single-college districts are grateful for the opportunities the college provides and proud of its standing in the community. The local newspaper, chamber of commerce, school districts, service clubs, and social media can be the college's strongest supporters when things are going well.

The attention a single-college district garners also means the political and social pressure can be intense. Everyone knows whom to turn to when decisive issues are broached or when a college employee gets caught, for example, scamming money from a student. If things go wrong, the local paper and social media know exactly whom to blame. And because the community college is *the* college in town, the town's movers and shakers expect the college leadership to take an active role in all affairs of the community.

If you are part of the administrative leadership of a single-college district, plan on joining one of the local service clubs. Connecting to the community becomes an important part of the job description, especially for vice presidents, presidents, and chancellors. Civic service, whether United Way or Rotary, can provide a valuable link to the community.

THE MULTICOLLEGE DISTRICT

The difference between a single-college district and a multicollege district is similar to the difference between having one child and having two. That second child, as well as the third and fourth, brings more joy but also more competition for your time, attention, and resources.

Adding just one accredited campus to a district changes the dynamics of how the CEO works, how the board operates, and even the jobs of campus vice presidents and middle managers. Inevitably, the challenge for multicollege district leaders becomes how to best allocate attention, time, and resources among the campuses. Unfortunately, if campus leaders are so inclined, the process can become even more complex—and combative—if the colleges are determined to battle over budget allocation, that is, small campus versus large campus or a campus with a high proportion of at-risk students versus a campus with a record of high academic achievement.

We've seen it all: campuses involved in internecine war with each other, with the district office, or with both; the small campus battling the flagship campus; the campuses battling the chancellor and board to minimize staff and resources in the "nonproductive" district office; or the district office, whose only constituency is the board of trustees, defending itself against allegations of being heavy-handed during budget deliberations, program planning, or facility planning.

The multicollege district is also often hampered by a related challenge: defining and justifying its role. Everyone knows what a college president does. But what does a chancellor, whose office may be in some business complex away from students and faculty, do? And how does she or he contribute to learning on the campuses?

Boards in multicollege districts also tend to be more volatile and political than single-college district boards, especially in urban areas. Boards in multicollege districts often are more responsive to internal politics and constituencies, particularly unions and senates. These board members don't hear much from the community but do get an earful from various campus interest groups who also can provide them with money and endorsements when they or their political patrons run for election.

In the big urban multicollege districts, boards, CEOs, and faculty leaders also deal with the current racial, sexual, and socioeconomic issues of the day. In many districts, campus politics are a reflection of the social and political issues swirling around the larger city and in American culture itself.

MULTICOLLEGE AND SINGLE-COLLEGE DISTRICTS

Issues for Administrators to Consider

Advantages

- Many multicollege districts can offer a wider scope of educational programs and services than can single-college districts.
- With campus presidents and administrators physically separated from the district office, campus educational leaders have more autonomy than at single-college district.
- More opportunities for economies of scale at multicollege districts.
- Often single-college districts are more united in purpose and identity than multicampus districts.
- Presidents of a single-college district have opportunity for coordinated and focused "speaking with one voice" relationship with the community.
- Because the day-to-day work of the colleges is handled on the campuses, the chancellor of a multicollege district may have more opportunity for community outreach.

- Presidents and campus administrators in a multicollege district can focus their efforts on their campus and its service area issues and needs without day-to-day interaction with the district board or statewide governing and regulatory agencies.

Disadvantages

- More CEO turnover at multicollege districts, creating challenges for entire management team.
- Longer tenure for middle management at multicollege districts can contribute to institutional stagnation.
- District office–campus relations are sometimes divisive and complex at multicollege districts, with the DO and chancellor playing the recurring role of the "bad guy."
- Sometimes tough, divisive budget battles break out between individual colleges and DO at multicollege districts.
- Often multicollege district trustees "adopt" or advocate for one college/campus over another college/campus, causing management headaches and challenges.
- Politics at the board level in multicollege districts often reflect the racial, cultural, and gender politics of the larger community and its culture.
- Single-college district CEO must be the face of the college in the community but also is busy with day-to-day campus issues.
- Chancellor has to coordinate, or keep control, of outreach to the community by campus presidents to ensure minimum overlap and tension with political, education, and community leaders.

RAM AND "BUCKET" BUDGET MODELS

Some districts across the country have come up with some interesting budget allocation models to mitigate the struggle between campuses and the traditional struggles within collective bargaining contracts, especially at multicollege and multicampus college districts.

Resource allocation model or RAM—This strategy deals with allocating campus resources based on historical enrollments and staffing but actively adjusted at set intervals (i.e., every two years). For example, if a campus grows in a certain time period, it would receive additional resources whereas a campus that loses enrollment would have some of their resources redistributed.

The "Bucket" budget model—Money is set aside for salaries and other collective bargaining needs (such as health benefits) based on enrollment, faculty load, and average class size.

THE MULTICAMPUS COLLEGE DISTRICT

In the multicampus college district, each campus is comprehensive in educational scope and facility infrastructure. The multicampus college district generally has some distinct administrative advantages over its cousin, the multicollege district. First, its name is associated with a well-known educational institution, such as Maricopa Community College. (In a multicollege district, the colleges have names entirely different than the name of the district.) Second, the CEO is seen as the sole educational leader of the district since he or she leads both the campuses and a district. As a result, the administrative structure in the district office can focus its efforts on managing and coordinating the educational goals of its campuses, not on breaking up turf wars among the colleges.

We believe most faculty members in multicollege districts think the district office suffers from a bloated administrative superstructure. We've sometimes found that this perception is correct. By their nature, multicollege districts are decentralized, whereas multicampus college districts are designed specifically to be centralized. We don't think a multicollege district needs a lot of administrators in the district office. We suggest you put your administrative resources in the colleges where they can make a difference. Otherwise, you end up having too many administrators and too many duplicated functions.

But a multicampus college district should be handled in just the opposite way. The central office of a multicampus college district has the same functions as that of a single-college district. Therefore, administrative resources should be put in the central office where they can manage the educational mission of the entire college in a coordinated, efficient manner.

THE NOMADIC LIFESTYLE

For many community college administrators, adopting the lifestyle of the professional nomad is part of the personal price paid for advancing a career.

We all know colleagues who have spent an entire career at one college, moving up the ranks, living in one home, building a large network of friends, paying off the mortgage, and getting to know their kids' friends. We know others who have chosen to move with the job. (The authors have worked in nine different districts in three different states.)

There are advantages to both lifestyle choices. If you're willing to move, the number and variety of jobs available for your consideration increase exponentially. If you stay put, you increase exponentially the chances that you'll pay off your mortgage. If you stay put, you will also find the options to moving up the ladder limited (especially if your boss never moves or you have to make a few too many no-win decisions).

As your administrative career unfolds, you will be forced to make a decision on which road to take: stay and advance up the local career ladder, or become a professional nomad and, in effect, cause a lifestyle change that will have an impact on your career and family. Table 1.1 might help you choose a path.

Table 1.1. To Move or Not to Move

Your Life	Moving	Not Moving
Job Opportunities	Quicker rise to top	Limited to local openings
Professional Accomplishments	Do more in many places	Do more in one place longer
Paycheck	Opportunity to pick best-paying colleges	Limited to local pay scale
Personal Career Needs	New, different challenges	Stability, predictability
Spouse	Problem if she or he is well established	May be better for marriage
Housing	Tough to pay off mortgage	Build home equity
Friends	Make more but lose more	Watch neighbor kids grow up
Your Kids	May resent changing schools	Stability in school and with friends

ARE SMALL-TOWN POLITICS REALLY EASIER?

> *In a town this size,*
> *There's no place to hide*
> *Everywhere you go*
> *You meet someone you know.*

—from the song "In a Town This Size"

Some community college administrators think politics in the large urban areas are more vicious than in the small, quiet, rural communities. Don't believe that for a second.

In the big city, you can hide a lot easier. You can get lost within the diversity of people and activities. In the big city the politics are more philosophical. In a small town they're more personal.

A college CEO we know in a rural, agricultural area lived through a bitter personal battle with a faculty member that would send cold shivers down the back of any urban administrator. The unhappy instructor, who thought the CEO was a crook and made no bones about telling the entire town, had no facts—only passion, anger, time, and resources (and tenure) to make the CEO's life and that of her family miserable. The campaign against the CEO, in this small, quiet community, included garbage tossed on her front yard and dead animals stuffed in her mailbox.

In another small, rural town, a prominent physician discovered that his wife—a student at the local community college—was having an affair with a member of the college faculty. When his demand for retribution fell on deaf ears in the college president's office, the doctor proceeded to plaster "Wanted for Adultery" posters all over town picturing the instructor. In a large city, those posters would have gotten lost among the billboards and graffiti. Not in Small Town, USA.

Some administrators will say, "But my personal life is no business of the college." Don't believe it for an instant. Did someone see you in a bar having too good a time? Why weren't you and your spouse together at the town's big social event? Whether or not that's anybody's business is not the issue. If you don't want to live in that kind of fishbowl, don't take a high-visibility job in that kind of community.

We recommend that you hit the banquet circuit if you ever do get to the small town. It's expected of the top leadership at the college and it's a great way to build relationships that will pay off later when you need help from the community. We also recommend you live in the district or service area your college serves. Inevitably, you will be out and about in the community and the question will arise, "So, where do you live?" It can only help your cause—professionally and personally—if you can answer, "In the same town as my students."

WORKING AT A SMALL-TOWN COLLEGE

Advantages

- Do a good job and you can be king or queen of not only the college but of the educational community.
- You're a big fish in a small pond with all the associated benefits.
- You have high visibility and respect as a college educator.
- You'll experience less sympathy in town for union issues/collective bargaining issues. (Small towns don't always countenance to faculty

complaining about working twenty hours a week while making more money than most civic leaders.)

Disadvantages

- Mess up and everyone knows it. Quickly.
- If your spouse or kids mess up, everyone knows it. Quickly.
- Community memory of college-related problems, controversies, and scandals last forever.
- The CEO has to deal with the problems of everyone on staff, up and down the ranks.

COMMUTER MARRIAGES

Would you give up living with your wife or husband for a job?

We know one couple—both of them top-level administrators—who lived apart for twenty years while the husband climbed the career ladder to the top at a faraway college. Another woman administrator we admire moved out of the house and into a different state to take her first presidency.

Extremes? Not exactly. In today's job market, where opportunity and advancement sometimes require personal sacrifices, the ability to be flexible can make a difference in how quickly you advance toward your professional goals. And because so many professional educators are married to other professionals, a dilemma arises when one or the other hears the siren call from another city or state.

This phenomenon can play out in different ways. Moving away from a spouse does put a strain on the relationship. There is no question that even loving, dedicated couples are negatively affected. It takes a special partnership to overcome not only the physical distance but the emotional separation.

While we have seen such separations work, we also know administrators who, when they move away from their spouse, end up throwing themselves into their jobs, believing that going overboard will compensate for an empty house. And, as we all know, long hours on the job do not equate with improved productivity or better judgment. Or happiness.

Moving to a job without your spouse can also become a political issue, especially in small towns where a high-visibility college administrator is assumed to be part of a married "team." It may be old-fashioned, but in many communities the standard is still the image of the Norman Rockwell family.

THE STING

We know a college where the board of trustees conducted interviews with prospective CEO candidates and their spouses and were particularly impressed with one of the candidates, Joe, and his wife, Sara Jean. She was a vivacious, intelligent woman who, the board agreed, would make Joe an even better college representative on the town-and-gown circuit. During the interview, Sara Jean aggressively sold Joe's candidacy. After being selected for the job, Joe arrived in town—without Sara Jean. He assured everyone she would be joining him within a few months. When months had passed, an embarrassed Joe announced that he and Sara Jean were getting a divorce. Only later did the board discover that Joe and Sara Jean, the perfect couple during the interviews, had filed for divorce six weeks before he even applied for the job.

2

Thriving and Surviving on the Job

WHAT ADMINISTRATORS REALLY DO

The notes I handle no better than many pianists. But the pauses between the notes—ah, that is where the art resides!

—Artur Schnabel

Imagine a community college district with the perfect set of board policies and administrative regulations: published documents that state exactly and clearly the goals and mission of the institution; how the board, faculty, administration, and support staff will function; the rules and limits for student activities; how budgets will be balanced; the curriculum and class schedule process; and so on.

This set of policies and regulations is so good, in fact, that whenever a decision or judgment is required—even those never before contemplated—college officials simply open the policies and regulations, turn to the index, and voila, find the answer within.

Welcome to the twilight zone.

The reality of community college leadership is that the written policies and regulations fit about 75 percent of the cases. There are always one or two situations a week that you won't find in the book. *Administrators are paid to adjudicate the gray areas and clarify the ambiguities—the other 25 percent.*

How do you accomplish this task when you are new to the job?

Start with understanding that ethical and consistent behavior—acting with integrity—fosters trust and a willingness on the part of people to respect your judgment and follow your lead. (*Begin with the personal core values*

19

addressed in section titled "Can It Pass the 'Do You Want Your Loved Ones to Know?' Test?" in chapter 3.)

Next, build on the work you have done reading the college's latest accreditation report and other key reports by getting out and talking to people at all levels of the campus community—your boss, peers, subordinates, and college staff—to discover the typical points of dispute and disagreement at your college and in your particular area. You'll find people like to talk, share information, and give their opinions on issues and challenges facing the institution. Just ask them!

Any job has responsibilities, but there are usually two or three issues facing your division or department or campus that fall within what we call the "gray areas" and must be handled tactfully. Don't ever assume you already know what all these issues are, regardless of your experience and expertise. Talking to a wide swath of people early on the job is a good way to get a jump on the key challenges you'll be facing.

When adjudicating the gray areas and clarifying the ambiguities, administrators and leaders would do well to follow these simple rules:

1. Understand and embrace the notion that your job as a leader is to provide, advocate for, and secure the resources and tools necessary for your team to get their jobs done.
2. Take charge. Risk the wrath of the people upstairs to get things done for faculty, staff, and students. Assume you have the authority to make the decisions that are needed until someone says you don't.
3. Take a commonsense approach to decision making. We don't need more "you have to dot the i's and cross the t's" administrators in the community colleges. We have plenty of them already.
4. Understand that the real action at a community college takes place at the department and division levels and that administrators are responsible for setting a tone that encourages teaching and learning. As a college president, you can have popular pizza parties and send out wonderful emails and texts and celebrate birthdays, but the morale and the institutional climate at a campus is determined by how effective the department chairs and division deans are in dealing with faculty and staff day-to-day needs.

Number 4 is particularly important. The effectiveness of the division and department leadership is critical to the college CEO or president. Too often the perception of how things are going at a college mistakenly begins and ends at the door of the top tier of campus leadership. In reality, the real action is at the department or division level. Vice presidents, presidents, and

CEOs would serve themselves well by placing a framed copy of the following statement in the middle of their desks as a friendly reminder of where most of their real problems actually begin: *What we perceive in upper management as small-potato issues are often perceived as big, hot potatoes in faculty offices.*

Delegate, delegate, delegate down. Too many managers worry that their employees are going to make big mistakes if given too much leeway or authority to make decisions. They're wrong. Ninety-five percent of the staff will do the right thing, especially if the administrator has done her or his job as a teacher and mentor. The other 5 percent who don't demonstrate good judgment or aren't responsible are the people who do have to be watched and need better mentoring and professional development or need your help to find a better fit elsewhere.

BUILDING CAREER BRIDGES

Have you noticed how frequently community college presidents and administrators move from one state to another for job opportunities? Or from one college to another within the same state? We've talked with presidents, for example, who have worked in three or four different states during a thirty-year career. We certainly know administrators who have worked at several colleges within the same state or even region.

There are nearly 1,500 community colleges in the United States, but our professional circles are rather small, especially when you go down to the state or regional level. It's not uncommon for administrators active in state associations and organizations of one sort or another to interact with administrators from a large number of college districts.

For a dean that is ambitious, it's a piece of information and insight worth keeping in mind.

As you begin your career, strive to build relationships that will benefit, and not hurt, you. When you go to a conference, or participate on a committee and especially when working with colleagues on your own campus, don't ever forget that of the many people you interact with during any academic year, it's inevitable that one or more may very well have a significant impact on your career someday in the future.

Someday, one or more of the same people you serve with on an accreditation team or whom you met at a state or national conference could be on a hiring committee you're sitting in front of seeking that next promotion. One of them could even be your boss in your next job.

Because you never know who exactly will appear in your future, it's a good idea to always strive to build bridges, not burn them. Getting on the wrong side of too many people early in your career could wind up sinking it before it gets off the ground.

WATCH WHAT YOU SAY OR DO . . .

When you are dealing with people that are power-players outside your professional circle, it is best to use the same protocols you do when dealing with powerful people that do work and live within your profession.

Let us give you an example.

We know a former college president who was at the apex of his career when the congresswoman who represented his college in the U.S. House of Representatives phoned to ask to come on campus to film a campaign commercial. As the president took the call, he thought back on all the years the congresswoman had failed to provide the support the college president believed was important to students. When the congresswoman asked permission to film the commercial, the president reminded her that she had, in his opinion, failed the college and that until she took action to support the college's federal initiatives, she was not welcome on campus.

Fast forward several years to an election in which several protégés of the congresswoman are running for seats on the community college board of trustees. We began this story by saying, we knew a former college president. You're probably way ahead of us . . . After the election and after the congresswoman's protégés were seated, they formed a majority that quickly removed the president from his position. In many professions, including politics and higher education, memories are long and, in many cases, unforgiving.

WINNING CHARACTERISTICS

Being part of management doesn't mean you have a hammer in your hand and that everything you see is a nail.

—Robert Jensen

As you move up the administrative ranks, you will come to realize that community college administration boils down to the inescapable fact that, in the end, it's all about people—how you treat them, how you react to them, and how you work with them.

Don't be like the CEO who let the relentless pressures of a campus dissident cloud her judgment and seriously hurt her credibility. The CEO had been taking intense criticism from one particular faculty member who was sending out regular anonymous campuswide "newsletters" packed with denunciations of the CEO. When these "newsletters" began to attack the CEO's spouse, the CEO, with the blessings of the board, hired a private investigator to uncover the culprit. Using a handwriting sample from the attack newsletter, the private investigator scoured the campus personnel files until he was able to match the sample with an old application form. The cowardly critic was unmasked! But the reaction wasn't what the CEO expected. The entire campus exploded in anger at the CEO and the board, demanding the "restoration of free speech" and an end to "dictatorial strong-arm tactics."

What does this mean to you? Several things:

- Don't take everything personally. Particularly, don't overreact to the handful of malcontents on campus. It will just stir up and possibly alienate all the people in the middle.
- Keep your door open. Answer your phone. People should come first. Take your paperwork home if you have to.
- Resist the temptation to be on every committee and to run off to every conference. Keep your eye on the ball at home.
- Be consistent and fair.
- Listen, listen, and listen some more.
- Socialize with your colleagues. If you play golf, find some golfing partners from the faculty and administrative staff. If you play bridge, find bridge players on campus.

We guarantee you'll have fewer personnel problems or disputes if your door is always open and if you listen, show interest and passion, and put your cards (or as many as possible) on the table. Too often administrators, like the Wizard of Oz, hide behind a curtain of paperwork and committee meetings to the detriment of faculty, students, and staff. Your job is to set the tone and goals, be the cheerleader and provide the energy necessary for success.

We were once standing in line to check baggage at an airline and watched in horror as a man in front of us gave the luggage handler in the airport a lot of grief. We mean a lot of grief. Berating and browbeating the poor handler about how he'd allegedly been subjected to the airline's lousy service. When the passenger finally left in a huff and it was our turn, we asked the baggage handler how he could put up with such treatment. The handler said matter-of-factly, "He's going to Chicago, but his luggage is going to Japan." The baggage handler didn't get mad; he got even.

The moral: treating people as second-class citizens is hurtful, unproductive, and unnecessary.

Whether it's your boss or the employees you supervise, treating people with kindness and honesty is important and, in the long run, beneficial to all.

THERE IS NO "MIDDLE" IN MIDDLE MANAGEMENT

The first thing you learn when you become an administrator, especially if you're coming from the faculty ranks, is that the First Amendment no longer applies.

—Pat Kirklin, retired faculty union leader and administrator

We hear people say, "Middle management is tough because you're caught in the middle between faculty and the president." Directors and deans complain, "I'm being pulled by faculty and staff in one direction and my boss and the CEO in another. I'm caught in the middle!" The fact is there is no "middle" in middle management.

When you sign on as an administrator, you give up part of your autonomy to be part of the administrative team, a team that has both benefits and expectations.

As you walk across that line into administration, you don't cross over a wide tract of no-man's-land dubbed "middle ground." You made a choice and in doing so you lost some of your autonomy and some of your professional and personal freedoms. If there are any tugs and pulls in loyalties, priorities, or goals, they are all in your mind, not in your job description. Your job description says "administration." Welcome to the club.

NOW GET OUT THERE AND STRETCH

Far too often, administrators move up the ranks through either instruction or student services or finance with little cross-fertilization in terms of professional experiences. It's a rare CEO who mentors his or her staff by shuffling the deck occasionally and making the players put on different hats and thus learn new skills. If you find yourself becoming a limited expert in student services, for example, do some cross-fertilization on your own by attending conferences of the instructional folks or business officials. This will give you a sense not only of the issues on their front burner but of the potential impact of those issues on your department.

DIVISION AND DEPARTMENT LEADERSHIP

The division dean—the classic "middle management" position in a community college—has a huge influence on the success or failure of a CEO. One reason is the morale and perceptions of the institution depends on how well the department and division leadership interacts with faculty. You, as a college president, can be extremely popular or successful. The board can love you. And so can the Kiwanis Club. But if the science department hates their dean and there's a war being fought down at the other end of campus, someone will inevitably ask the science faculty, "What's morale like in this institution?" and they're going to shout, "It's terrible!" And suddenly the instructional vice president and the CEO have a big problem.

Another reason the division dean is important is that the heart of any community college is a dedicated, talented, and diverse faculty and its class schedule—both the purview of division leadership.

A dedicated, talented, and diverse faculty interacts directly at the intersection of student learning, the primary mission of any institution of higher education.

And the class schedule determines, in part, whether a college is meeting its education mission and can be accessed by the community. The class schedule also drives the budget.

Now, the toughest job a division dean has is developing a class schedule and deciding which classes will be offered and when. Faculty members can be bulldogs when it comes to teaching the classes they want on the dates and times they want. The dean may be tempted to delegate this responsibility, often to a department chair. The class schedule, however, should serve student needs and not be built solely around instructor convenience. Therefore, you have to hire division deans who are tough enough not to cave in to inappropriate, self-serving, and/or costly instructor demands.

But division and department leaders must also focus on building and supporting the needs of a diverse faculty and support staff that reflects, as much as possible, the racial, cultural, and sexual diversity of the student body and larger community. We believe student success flourishes in such a campus environment.

The college CEO who delegates the hiring of these frontline administrators—division and department leaders—to his vice presidents not only misses an opportunity to protect his own best interests, but more important, misses the chance to help set the course for the institution's future. The legacy of a college CEO is not bricks and mortar. It's people, including "middle" managers.

COMMUNICATION ON CAMPUS

Where is the knowledge we have lost in information?

—T. S. Eliot

An important role for any administrator on a community college campus is communicating up the line with senior leadership, across the organization with fellow middle managers, and down the line with staff and faculty. Middle management acts somewhat like the server in a computer network. It works as the link through which data, dialogue, information, and opinions travel from one end of the campus to the other. Therefore, the information management provides through the campus network must be accurate and complete, and the opinions communicated must be based on good judgment.

Effective communication is critical in order to build a strong team and move an agenda, regardless if you're a dean, a vice president, or the college president. And we always need to remember there are two components to good communication—listening to and facilitating communication. (We're all pretty good at talking but too few of us have honed the equally important skill of listening.)

Good communication also requires that management's professional relationships and credibility with faculty, staff, and senior management are solid. Your word will be heard and taken seriously only if you are, first of all, trusted and respected. Being liked also helps. (Having a personal rapport with your staff is like money in the bank when tough news needs to be delivered.) To be a leader, you have to have followers.

How can you as a manager obtain accurate information? Assume that the table of organization acts like a communication filtration system. As information is passed around, people tend to put a coat of sugar—or vinegar—on it as it befits their own political, professional, and personal interests. Therefore, you must constantly check to guarantee the accuracy of the information you receive and the information you pass along.

Here are some things to remember about communication:

- A top communication priority for managers is keeping your immediate team and boss up-to-date and informed on important campus and department issues.
- It is critical that you maintain your integrity and credibility with your team, including staff, faculty, and administrators. If you don't, you lose your ability to lead.
- Deans should constantly communicate with faculty and staff to ensure the accuracy of their own perceptions. Identify a small cadre of faculty

and staff—folks we call "touchstones"—that you can go to for insider, accurate information on what's really going on in your areas.

- Emails, texts, and memos are forms of passive communication and are not a substitute for in-person, active interaction.
- Data is not equivalent to information.

And please note, delivering bad news to the president or your immediate supervisor is a tough but essential role for the college administrator. Your boss needs to hear it from you before she hears it from others in the organization or outside the chain of command. And what about bad news regarding the CEO or one of his pet projects? It may be uncomfortable to tell the boss "this isn't playing well with the troops," but it's part of your job, just as it is part of the president's job to listen and learn. But be prepared to offer suggestions and possible solutions for the situation at hand . . . not just pass along the message.

Putting the other shoe on, as a supervisor or CEO receiving bad news, it helps if you don't come off as defensive and paranoid. A boss who shoots the messenger will quickly get shut off from the flow of information. In the preface of this book, we told the story of a highly respected community college leader who was blindsided by some bad news that ended up costing him his reputation and job. He had become one of those bosses who often "shot" the bearers of bad news. As a result, the business manager, who had prayed he'd never have to deliver the bad news, held on to the time bomb until the college had a major fiscal/budget problem that finally exploded all over everyone.

Some other important communication points:

- The less your administrative team communicates with the larger campus community, the more power the gossipers and dissidents wield within the organization. Don't leave a communication void that others will be too happy to fill.
- Too many administrators spend too much of their time in meetings and hallways and back rooms whining about the way things are going, but then, when the president or their supervisor walks in the room, suddenly suffer from amnesia and talk about how everything is hunky-dory. This kind of behavior doesn't help you, the president, your supervisor, or the college. And we don't think it leaves your fellow managers with a lot of confidence and respect for you or in your word or your backbone.

Finally, people are incredibly busy these days, overwhelmed with texts, emails, the internet, phone calls, and doing their job. To protect themselves and to control the barrage of messages, college staff are increasingly putting their phones on automatic answering mode while sitting at their desk. "Sally

Jones is busy. But she really wants to hear from you. Please leave your name and a brief message . . ." The result? Faculty, staff, students, or the community are, in effect, being pushed away and told, "I'm too busy to deal with you."

When the phone on your desk rings a couple times before someone else in the office can answer it . . . pick it up yourself!

BRING OPTIONS, NOT JUST PROBLEMS

A manager who brings a problem to his or her boss without options or recommendations for addressing the issue is really just an overpaid messenger.

If the problem or challenge is in your area, you're responsible not only for identifying it but for finding solutions. The president or vice president should advise you on the validity of the solution, not be solely responsible for developing the solution or strategy.

We like working with people who begin their report on a problem or new idea like this: "I've got an idea for increasing enrollment in the social sciences. I've worked on this with my department chairs and have run it by a couple of my fellow deans. I'd like to get your ideas, as well. But first, let me outline briefly the enrollment challenge we're facing and some ideas for turning it around . . ."

INSTITUTING CHANGE: EVERYONE IS A LEADER

Change is not an easy thing for human beings. Change agents are not necessarily always your favorite person.

—Bob Herbold, Microsoft

When it comes to change, we don't practice what we preach in the community colleges. For example, the typical community college catalog includes a mission statement that may read, in part, something like this:

- Our college is dedicated to meeting the dynamic needs of a changing community.
- We seek to empower students to formulate and realize educational goals which will promote their personal growth and facilitate their full participation in a rapidly changing world.
- Our campus will establish, monitor, and evaluate college goals and objectives in relation to the mission and a changing environment.

But despite our allegiance (at least in writing) to change and helping students and the community prepare for new challenges, we tend to resist and even reject change when it comes to how we serve students and do our own jobs.

The Italian political philosopher Niccolò Machiavelli could have been commenting on the prejudice against change in the present-day community college when he wrote:

> There is no more delicate matter to take in hand, nor more dangerous to conduct, nor more doubtful of success, than to step up as a leader in the introduction of change. For he who innovates will have for his enemies all those who are well off under the existing order of things, and only lukewarm support in those who might be better off under the new.

But change is inevitable, whether we resist it or whether we welcome it. As the COVID pandemic of 2020 showed, college administrators open to and willing to make the necessary adjustments guided their institutions successfully through the crisis.

And anyone on a community college campus can be a leader when it comes to promoting change. It doesn't matter whether you're a custodian, a president, an instructor, or whether you work in the admissions and records office or sit on the board of trustees. Everyone can be an advocate for change.

For a board of trustees, change is easy: Get a new CEO. Or, better yet, work with your current CEO on developing definable goals and objectives to promote a new and better way of doing things.

For CEOs and presidents, things become a bit more complicated. A CEO or president must build a diverse chorus of people singing from the same song book as an essential first step. Defining the vision is the first step, but getting others to embrace and articulate that vision on the job becomes the most critical and challenging step in the change process.

Intuit, a pioneer of PC finance and tax software, addressed the need for change by involving a broad cross-section of employees. Ten percent of its headquarters staff were recruited to design a new internet strategy. The six months of deliberations appeared sometimes chaotic, but once the team settled on a strategy, its members became evangelists for change. "To succeed," Intuit CEO Scott Cook said, "you need people who have a whole bunch of passion, and you can't just order someone to be passionate about a business direction." The same holds true for a community college. The CEO has to involve folks in developing the mission and then get broad buy-in from the total institution.

Moving an agenda and playing pool have similar strategies. Sure, you can sink the first ball, but more important, where does the cue ball end up after the shot? You don't want to just sink the first shot. You want to run the table.

Smart administrators anticipate and strategize shots—or steps—down the line in order to lay the groundwork for future success. Ask yourself, what will the future consequences or scenarios be from your decision today? How will it affect the various departments or divisions involved? What are the potential political consequences? Budget impacts?

Remember, whether small or major, all decisions potentially have one or more of these three elements: an educational, fiscal, or political impact. Ignore this at your own peril.

THE LESSONS OF THE COVID EPIDEMIC (AND OTHER DISASTERS)

Whether it's an epidemic sweeping the nation or local or state disasters such as hurricanes, fires, or earthquakes, college leaders at all levels must be prepared for unexpected crisis. A crisis does not change what is expected of leaders: helping the campus community make decisions and giving them the resources necessary to succeed. Here are some questions and comments to help get ready for the unanticipated:

- Are your staff and faculty training systems strong enough to adapt quickly but appropriately to the consequences of the disaster? Can the college adjust if necessary to a sudden demand, for example, for more online courses?
- Is your technology, and specifically your website, the very latest and user-friendly for today and tomorrow's smartphone users (i.e., students, faculty, and staff)?
- Does your administrative team have the trust of the faculty and staff before disaster hits, after which quick and often unilateral steps will need to be taken to continue to provide what the community expects: accessible services and learning?
- Will your shared governance processes serve the interests of the institution under sudden stress?
- Are you prepared as an administrative team to act without the immediate direction of state or regional authorities?
- Are you prepared to ensure that you protect the health and safety of the college community?

Warning: Faculty and support staff and the administrative staff will, at first, be more flexible to change in order to respond to the crisis but will, after the initial shock has passed, demand a return to more "normal" college functions.

HIRING AND MANAGING A CONSULTANT

We like consultants. In fact, we've done some consulting ourselves. Having sat on both sides of the table, we know the valuable role consultants can play as well as the problems they can create if not managed properly.

What we like best about consultants is they can provide a skill set or experience that supplements the skills already available on campus. They can bring a third-party perspective and experience to a problem that provides the college real value-added benefits in planning, implementation, or evaluation.

The right consultants can also bring with them the authority of a "respected outside expert." Former presidents and vice presidents often can make a good living—and provide a valuable service—bringing their well-earned professional authority to a college facing difficult problems or needing a fresh perspective on an issue. Here are some reasons for hiring a consultant:

- To bring a specific skill or experience to a project that is not available on campus.
- To bring a third-party, objective perspective without political "skin in the game."
- To be the messenger of bad or politically sensitive news.

This last reason is particularly appropriate for a CEO new to the job who discovers some major weakness within the campus or district structure, particularly if it's related to the education program. Faculty are hypersensitive to new CEOs delivering the message that they are not doing a job as well as the last CEO kept telling them. It may be smarter not to expend the political capital necessary to get the message out but use it, instead, on eventually solving the problem. (*For more on expending political capital, see section "The Theory of Political Capital" in chapter 4.*)

Consultants can, if properly managed, also say or do something you as an administrator or trustee want them to say or do. We know a CEO who arrived at her new campus and discovered the education program had been happily stuck in the mud for several years. Wisely, she chose not to make the announcement public but to hire a consultant to conduct an analysis of the curriculum, how it was being offered, and its effectiveness in meeting community needs. The consultant became the bearer of bad news, and the CEO expended her energy (and political capital) to get the education program out of the mud.

The biggest mistake administrators make when hiring a consultant involves letting them loose without any clear direction or parameters. If a consultant has been brought in to deal with a sensitive, politically charged issue, the last thing you want is a freelancer walking around campus lifting rocks you don't want turned over or bringing home stuff you don't want delivered. So before you bring in the consultants, be sure you're clear in your own mind what you want. And before giving them the keys to the campus, be sure in your planning meeting with your consultants you provide them with specifics and details on

- The scope of issue to be addressed.
- What you expect from them.
- The process and techniques they will use.
- Who has final editing rights on the final draft of any reports. (You.)
- The campus and community politics involved in the issue being addressed.
- The relevant key players and opinion makers on campus.
- The "no surprises" rule: you want to meet with them regularly to discuss their findings and progress.

And beware of the consultant bearing the one-size-fits-all boilerplate solution. These are the ones who bring a solution they just used at another college that is as similar to yours as the Beatles are to Beethoven. A good way to prevent this disaster is to check all references carefully before a contract is signed.

Remember, you don't always have to use their report or abide by their recommendations. You may end up saying to them, "It's valuable information and something for me to think about but I'm not taking it outside this room." And then you say, in a polite way, "Now, go out and praise the college for its courage and foresight for studying this issue."

A UNIQUE WAY TO USE A TRUSTED OUTSIDE ADVISOR

We knew a chief business officer who used a clever, and cost-free, technique for getting outside input from a valued professional.

The CBO had a business relationship with a consultant who worked in the field of office building heating/air conditioning systems. The CBO trusted this professional to be honest, smart, and a good judge of people.

Struggling with the question of whether to hire a certain architect—a totally separate field from the HVAC business—the CBO decided to get input on his hiring decision from a businessperson he trusted, the HVAC pro.

He asked the HVAC pro to attend a meeting with the architect.

"But I don't know anything about this field."

"Just come and listen."

After the meeting, when the architect had left, the CBO turned to his guest and asked, "Would you trust this guy?"

"No, I wouldn't," said the HVAC consultant.

"That's what I thought," the CBO replied. "I just wanted a second opinion from someone I trust. Thanks."

ADJUSTING TO A CHANGING OF THE GUARD

When a new CEO comes on board, adjustments are required of everyone who works closely with the new boss. It's a time especially for trustees and administrators to lay aside past practices and open their minds to new ways.

We know a CEO hired by a large district who brought to her new job a philosophy of working closely and openly with all members of the board. Sounds refreshing and productive. Who would object to that? In this case, the new board chair. She had just been elected to the chair after six years as a trustee watching as the previous CEO focused all his attention on each succeeding board chair. The new chair wanted the new CEO to operate in the same manner. "I've been waiting to be the center of attention," she seemed to be saying, "and now you've changed the rules and I don't like it." The CEO who encountered the unhappy board chair needed to meet the problem head on.

Ideally, the issue of how the CEO and board work together as the district leadership team should be discussed thoroughly during initial selection interviews. But if a problem persists, the new CEO needs to set aside time with the board to give the issue the attention it requires. A good, clean "takeoff" is in everyone's best interest.

A new CEO also poses a challenge for the vice president who was an unsuccessful candidate for the top job. This situation can be stressful and threatening to both sides if not handled correctly. Don't run and hide from it. The vice president should take the lead and sit down with the new boss, shut the door, and talk it through. Is this going to work? How are we going to deal with it? Both parties have to be as honest as possible and make some decisions and adjustments.

However, if the VP does not step forward, the new CEO should handle this directly by emphasizing how valuable the vice president can be and expressing respect for their expertise and background and let them know you hope they will join the new team so that you can *all* be successful.

The smartest thing the vice president can do is to get behind the new president and make him or her successful. If you missed out on the top job, your long-term career aspirations will not be energized or your reputation enhanced by your sulking around campus complaining about the new president. Your colleagues won't respect you. The board won't respect you. And you'll probably just end up cooking your own goose. Remember, your new CEO will be writing your references for your next job—thumbs up or down.

The directors and deans on campus play a key role as well in the transition of a new president. When a new CEO comes on board, people look up the line for signals on how things are going with the new boss. Directors and deans have the opportunity through their attitudes and words to set a positive tone with staff and faculty. A positive comment can give the new CEO a chance to move the college forward. A roll of the eyes sends a signal that can undermine the new president and college leadership, including your own position as a member of that leadership team.

3

Institutional Politics

PEER BULLIES

We know an instructor who attended a weeklong, out-of-state conference without authorization from her dean and then bullied her peers into defending her unauthorized absence. The president ordered the dean, who had been on vacation, to write a letter of reprimand and put it in the instructor's personnel file.

The guilty faculty member responded by immediately filing a grievance, alleging that the rules for conference participation had been "secretly" changed. The instructor then cajoled several of her faculty colleagues to send letters to the faculty union saying a letter of reprimand was too severe a punishment. Instead of just saying no to their guilty colleague, the faculty members agreed to mail their letters, admitting afterward that taking the path of least resistance was preferable to standing up to a pushy colleague.

Peer bullies come in all shapes and sizes. We were attending a faculty union meeting at a large urban district at which the topic of the funding of health benefits was being discussed. One faculty leader—Joe—argued for taking no action to help administration address the issue. Another faculty leader—Sarah—argued that faculty should work with administration toward a reasonable solution. Joe's reaction was to grab the microphone out of Sarah's hand, jump up on the stage and attempt to win the argument by literally shouting her down.

We have been amazed at how easily faculty members are intimidated by colleagues who have no authority over them or who sometimes don't even work in the same department. Often, they know these peer bullies are wrong, probably have only half the story right, and are still afraid to stand up and take them on. Why do they get away with it?

As we all know, most people don't like confrontation. And in cases where an issue arises on which a faculty member has few facts, it's often easier to accede to what the bully says or demands than to take the time to research the issue or take a stand that is contrary to union or senate practices.

Many faculty members do not want to get involved. We call them "tweeners": people in the middle "between us and them." Their motto is, "I don't want to be on the senate. I don't have the ego needs. I don't need the stress. I just want to teach my classes and go home." As a result, they leave a vacuum for those who do have the interest, time, energy, and, too often, nonproductive or even inimical motives.

Peer bullies pose a threat to college administration. Administrators often calculate—sometimes wrongly—that the bully has a big following, so they cave in to peer bully demands.

It's a simple fact: peer bullies thrive in a campus environment lacking healthy communication between administrators and faculty.

The best advice we can give is not to cave in when a peer bully threatens you. Faculty members know who the cheap shot artists are among their peers. If they know you know and you don't do anything about it, you'll lose respect.

The best remedy? Adopt the sunshine theory. Expose the bullies to the sunshine of facts by being honest and consistent with your colleagues. Bullies thrive by distorting the issues and counting on inaccessible administrators to cache information.

However, there's something else for you to watch out for: the snake in the grass. They're easy to spot. They are the faculty, staff, or administrators who sit quietly while you're having an unpleasant confrontation with the bullies and then come up to you afterward and say, "We're right behind you, Sally. We really don't support what that jerk is saying about you. So don't take it personally."

Don't trust them for a second.

THE 10/90 RULE

Ten percent of the faculty speak for—or at least try to give the impression they speak for—90 percent of the faculty.

In reality, most full-time faculty care mainly about four issues: what they teach, when they teach, what classroom they teach in, and whether they get adequate compensation. And let's not forget office accommodations and parking. Their attitude, and a healthy one at that, is: Get out of my way and let me teach my classes and don't give me a bunch of bureaucratic nonsense.

What does that mean for college administrators? You need to cultivate relationships so that you can read the real intentions and interests of the general faculty. (*Remember what we said in chapter 2 about "touch-stones" in the faculty and staff.*) Building relationships with faculty helps you understand whether discontented faculty members actually do have a constituency backing them up or are just solo pilots trying to shoot you down.

THE IMPORTANCE OF LOYALTY

We knew a campus president who found it just about impossible to work co-operatively with the new chancellor of his multicollege district. It turned out the president had been an unsuccessful candidate for the chancellorship and now he was letting his disappointment turn into bad behavior.

He took to playing the martyr role acted out by campus presidents in too many multicollege districts: "I tried to get our campus its fair share," the college president would tell his administrators and faculty when he came back from meetings at the district office, "but the chancellor believes the other campuses deserve more than ours." And he persisted in his disappointment, eventually turning it into defiance.

Decisions that were agreed upon in district cabinet meetings were scorned when the president got back on his campus. Directions the chancellor gave—and that had been accepted at the district cabinet meetings—were ignored. Board members heard stories from the campus about how the chancellor, whose office was off campus, failed to understand campus educational issues.

The punch line to this story came after the president had left his job and a few years later applied for a job in a neighboring state. A friend of his former boss, who was a chancellor in that same neighboring state, heard this disloyal person was now a candidate for a local job and went out of his way to squash the application. He had known the president's management style and didn't want to see this kind of unprofessional behavior move into his neck of the woods.

Loyalty is a valuable asset in community college governance and administration. Without it, trust among colleagues, including the CEO and board team, is nearly impossible. Without trust, the decision-making process is virtually unworkable and long-term friendships are out of the question.

In a multicollege district it's absolutely essential that the campus presidents agree with the chancellor's agenda. We've seen too many multicampus or multicollege districts get sidetracked and chancellors bushwhacked by campus presidents with their own agendas. In a single-college district, the need to have the vice presidents and the deans on the same page becomes important. In either case, second-tier administrators who feel no connection to the boss can go through the motions and slow the program down or even stop it all together.

Here's our take on how loyalty should flow within our organizations:

1. *Loyalty of the board to the CEO.*
   The board has a vested interest in the success of its CEO and presidents. Their success shines directly on the trustees. Loyalty to a CEO comes from the outgrowth of a successful working, and often personal, relationship between trustees and their top administrator. Good working and personal relations empower the CEO to move the college forward, even in tough times or while under fire from critics.

   Without loyalty to the CEO, boards are stuck with a high-salaried, do-nothing administrative leader, afraid to make one false move. Furthermore, it's nearly impossible to build teamwork and loyalty among second- and third-tier administrators when CEOs are constantly being criticized by trustees or run in or out of office. Administrators begin asking themselves, "If I get behind this CEO and he leaves, what will happen to me? Will there be retribution against me because I supported the CEO? Will the group who ran off the CEO then come after me?"

2. *Loyalty of the CEO to the board.*
   One of the key barometers of a healthy board/CEO relationship is the willingness of the board at times to step up and speak out on behalf of the CEO when a tough decision must be made. The same is true, of course, of the CEO, who must advocate on behalf of the board when trustees are making difficult decisions. It's in the best interest of the board, the CEO, and the college if the board/CEO team hangs together in tough times.

   From the CEO perspective, you work for them. You need their support to be successful. But if for some reason you don't respect them, the relationship is doomed and you better get out before they catch on.

   And, Dr. CEO, don't go to conferences and badmouth your board. If you complain to colleagues about your board, you can just about guarantee one or more of your trustees is going to eventually hear about it from one of their trustee pals at other colleges. If you have a problem with your board or a particular member, talk it out face to face. You would expect no less if the tables were turned.

3. *Loyalty of chancellors and presidents to other administrators.*
Your administrative team, as we point out repeatedly in this book, is a chancellor's or president's best hope for a successful term in office. Treating the members of your team with respect and compassion will go a long way toward improving your chances of seeing your vision for the institution implemented. Here are a few things to remember:

- Respect and honor the differences in individual team members' personality, skills, and talent.
- Don't take everyone on your staff to the woodshed when you have just one culprit. Deal directly with the person at fault.
- Don't badmouth your administrators to others. It's tacky, unprofessional, and makes you look petty and small.
- Never, ever pick a "favorite" on your team and set them apart from the others. It's only natural that some will shine brighter. Just don't be obvious.

4. *Loyalty of administrators to their chancellor or president.*
If you can't support your leader's position, you have three choices: try to change your boss's point of view, support the boss, or get out. In the real world, of course, most people stay put. Therefore, administrators must work within the decision-making process, never shying away from arguing a contrary position, but ultimately supporting the president's decision.

Don't go into the president's office and badmouth a colleague. That's usually not well received by top brass. For one thing, the president might jump to the conclusion that you say the same things about her when you're in someone else's office.

The world of community colleges is a small world. If you are fairly well-known yourself, our bet is that you are one or two degrees of separation from every community college administrator in your state and maybe even the nation.

Our point? Don't carelessly complain or bad-mouth other people, including your boss. That saw cuts both ways. It will inevitably get back to them and could end up having an impact on your career—maybe not today but someday in the not-too-distant future. If you ever plan to apply for another job, particularly if it's at another campus, the people to whom you have been rude, disloyal, hurtful, or disrespectful are only a phone call away from the person doing the reference checks. You'll find it difficult, if not impossible, to outrun your professional reputation.

Bottom line: success of the district CEO and the college "raises all boats," enhancing your reputation and future career prospects.

DON'T FORGET SUPPORT STAFF

The men and women who serve as administrative assistants, custodians, clerks, technicians, and supervisors are invaluable not only to the smooth operation of a college but to the image projected by the college to students and the community. Support staff interact with the public on a daily basis, whether it be students looking for help on campus or potential students and the public seeking information.

It has long been our view that, more than any employee group, support staff deserve to be thought of as the most loyal and dedicated employees on campus.

Faculty leaders, administrators, and trustees should take care not only to treat support staff with respect but to encourage staff development initiatives whenever possible.

Administrative assistants can make or break you, especially as a college CEO. They usually have a firm grasp on reality, work hard, perform as good diplomats, and possess a sense of history that is invaluable. We've had a couple of administrative assistants who, if a college education had been available to them in their earlier days, would be giving us orders today. We've had admins who could juggle ten tasks at a time and smile warmly when you handed them an eleventh.

But we also once knew a chancellor who berated his administrative assistant, a seasoned pro who had already been on the job for many years when he arrived. His badgering forced her into early retirement. The next year she ran for a seat on the board of trustees. Well, you know where this story is going. It wasn't too many years later that she was on the majority side of a vote to force his early retirement.

Support staff are the glue that keep the ship together and row it forward day to day. Administrators—particularly CEOs—come and go, but support staff, cornerstones of our institutions, remain, putting their indelible mark on the campus.

CAN IT PASS THE "DO YOU WANT YOUR LOVED ONES TO KNOW?" TEST?

Community college administrators, faculty, and trustees face potential ethical quagmires on a regular basis. Tough, complex decisions, conflicting demands on resources and priorities, the quest for power and the need for achievement and recognition, decisions on multi-million-dollar contracts and the sexual tension among men and women working together late into the night and away from home generate innumerable hazards and temptations for the ethically challenged.

- We know a college CEO who was propositioned by the board chair. He, the CEO, was single, and she was separated from her husband. After a late-night board meeting, she suggested that instead of going to a local restaurant to have a beer and talk about the meeting, they go to her house and have a drink. One thing led to another—the proposition, the acceptance, and the inevitable outcome.
- An instructor, desperate to make his class go, enrolled students without their permission and then proceeded to "forget" what he had done. When he subsequently noticed these students were failing to come to class, he was outraged and gave them a failing grade. His scam came undone when the students complained to the dean after receiving their grades.
- A board of trustees hired a CEO to balance the budget and rein in out-of-control employee pay and benefits. When the CEO did her job and employee groups complained bitterly to the board and to the media about the "CEO's lack of commitment to quality education," the board said to the CEO, "Hold it, what are you doing, Dr. CEO? People are unhappy! You've got to make them happy or you're out of here!" Elected or appointed officials can be fickle, especially if it affects their political reputations and prospects.
- A seventy-nine-year-old instructor, no longer effective in the classroom but a guaranteed plaintiff in a racial and age discrimination lawsuit if steps were ever taken to force his retirement, stayed on the job. Should faculty, who demand respect for their classroom and education pedagogy, stand up and demand the termination of instructors who are hurting students? What about the instructor's dean? When does inviting a lawsuit become the right thing to do?
- We also know of a situation where a college president billed the district for travel that on paper was for attendance at an important education conference, but in reality it was a trip to Las Vegas for some old-fashioned unwholesome fun. The president dug his hole deeper by using his college-issued phone to make long-distance calls to a sex-worker in a nearby city. A classified employee in the college business office—responsible for paying all phone bills—caught him red-handed.

We are faced with ethical misbehavior and dilemmas almost every day. No doubt you can cite examples from your own professional experience: faculty who have sex with students, administrators who sell life insurance out of their offices, presidents who bring their spouses to cabinet meetings, deans who hire relatives, and trustees who take campaign money from employee groups or try to get their romantic partners hired. The student is an adult, says the faculty member. The administrator is selling life insurance on his own time. And, yes, the trustee pockets the campaign contributions but she also promises to keep the institution's best interests in mind when voting on employee pay raises. Conflicts of interest? Ethical misbehavior? You bet.

You may not be able to teach people honest, ethical behavior, but there is a simple test that will help you spot poor behavior or resist it when it tempts you. We call it the "Do You Want Your Loved Ones to Know?" test:

1. Would you want your spouse, kids, parents, or neighbors to read about it in tomorrow's paper?
2. Is it how you would want to be treated?
3. Is it consistent with your values?

Unethical behavior diminishes the institution and its leadership in the eyes of the campus community and the general public. The college CEO, in particular, occupies a unique position in the ethical life of the institution—the center of the moral life of the college. How the CEO personally behaves and responds to the behavior of others sets a campuswide standard and example. When he or she behaves ethically and consistently over a period of time, it creates a campus environment that enhances the CEO's ability to make tough decisions on sticky issues and still maintain the support of the campus, even if the decisions are opposed by powerful forces.

The stench of poor ethical behavior has a "life cycle" that is long and destructive, potentially affecting enrollments and community support, both fiscally and politically, for years and years.

SHARED GOVERNANCE:
THE CONTRADICTION WE LOVE TO HATE

We spend too much time arguing over who's going to drive the bus and not enough time thinking about the passengers.

—Robert Jensen

A college president we know decided to make shared governance— collaborative decision-making involving representatives of the various groups on campus—work on his campus by creating an advisory committee of campus leaders (faculty, support staff, students, and administrators) to review all major issues and make recommendations to the president's council.

The advisory committee took him up on his offer, meeting once a week, discussing and debating issues, and struggling with the myriad points of view that major issues tend to generate. And then the headaches began.

When the advisory committee brought their decisions to the president and his council of vice presidents and deans, some of their recommendations were politely but firmly rejected. Rightly or wrongly, the advisory committee members concluded they had been misled and duped. "Why ask for our hard work and opinions if they're going to be dismissed?" they complained. "What do you know that we haven't already considered? Is this shared governance or is this is a benevolent despot? The voice of the faculty is not respected at this institution!"

Shared governance is a continuing tension for many community colleges. The effort to expand the circle of decision makers across the campus raises a dust storm of controversy on the question of where the buck actually starts and stops.

This is our view on shared governance: we believe the board of trustees has ultimate responsibility for deliberating on the recommendations of the CEO and making decisions in the best interest of the institution. We often forget that boards, not campus committees or CEOs, are empowered to hire and fire and make policy. The CEO is empowered to ensure the board receives a comprehensive presentation on the issue under consideration and a recommendation that, if approved by the board, will serve the college well. The CEO also has a responsibility to solicit from his or her administrative staff, and the appropriate members of the campus community, information, insights, ideas, and opinions on all major issues coming before the board.

If, as we believe, one of the greatest weaknesses of collaborative decision-making stems from the lack of understanding on campus of how the process works, administrators, and particularly presidents and chancellors, must take the blame. We would be willing to wager that most community college employees have no common concept of how decisions are made and who is involved. That general campuswide lack of knowledge breeds misunderstanding and suspicion and makes decision makers vulnerable to the second guessers, gossipers, and dissidents.

It is imperative that the institution's board and administrative leadership make clear to everyone on campus how decisions evolve and the roles of the people and groups involved. When campus committees are given a clear statement of responsibilities, expectations, and ground rules, others will have difficulty hoodwinking and manipulating the system.

We do believe in the collaborative involvement of all the appropriate staff and faculty groups, if it adds value. If you're discussing technology infrastructure planning, you shouldn't take a Noah's Ark approach to appointing a campus committee to develop a plan. Leave the "two from every group" approach for the feel-good issues. For the technology infrastructure committee, appoint faculty and staff with technology expertise. If you have more staff than faculty that can bring value to the process, bite the bullet and appoint more staff than faculty. What counts here are results, not politically correct body counts.

Now, what mistake did our friend make by asking his advisory committee to meet and deliberate on all major issues facing the college? Certainly, his intentions were good. However, in this day of raised decision-making expectations, if you appoint an advisory committee and charge them with going through the hard work of studying and building consensus on issues, you had better be prepared to follow their recommendation or take a lot of flak. Human nature being what it is, if you keep asking for advice and then keep rejecting it, you'll be seen either as obstinate or hard of hearing. Be careful with shared governance committees. They have the potential to encircle and outnumber the president, sandwiching him between the committee and his own cabinet and board.

One other thing: the campus wallet will take a big "hit" in order to maintain a multilayered governance structure that includes a president's cabinet with faculty and staff participation; a shared governance committee with faculty, staff, and management participation; as well as budget, curriculum, planning, and staff development committees. It is cumbersome, and release time for nonmanagers is expensive. (Most faculty would be up in arms if they knew how much release time was costing them in salary and benefits.)

Campus leaders must act to protect themselves and the process by defining decision making and governance, particularly to the faculty. If it means running the college, the answer is no. If it means having input into curriculum, the answer must be yes. But remember: whoever owns the curriculum process owns the budget. Scheduling determines costs, enrollment, hiring, and ultimately, budget. Don't give the faculty carte blanche or you'll lose control of the heart of the institution.

Bottom line: shared governance is an oxymoron. It's not in the job description of a committee to share accountability and responsibility. Just as you can't fire a last place football team, you can't fire a committee.

PEER REVIEW, FACULTY COP-OUT

One issue that does go hand-in-hand with the concept of shared governance is faculty peer review. Faculty represent themselves as experts on the subject of learning and teaching and have justifiably argued for years that they should exert "primacy" over curriculum decisions. It follows, therefore, that they, better than administrators, can assess the effectiveness of their fellow instructors in the classroom through the evaluation process, or peer review.

As a department or division dean, don't bet on that ever happening. Faculty may believe in the integrity of the teaching profession and the sanctity of the classroom, but when it comes to peer review, few in the club seem to be willing to expose ineffective instructors and risk opening up a messy debate on standards. Or anger their peers.

When was the last time your campus fired an ineffective instructor, even one that everyone knew was hurting students? Why? Part of the reason is the confluence of interests of the faculty union and the academic senate. Senates, which are responsible for representing faculty on academic issues, often join with the union, which represent dues-paying members on employment-related issues, in a one-two punch against the authority of administrators, even in the case of an incompetent instructor.

4

Presidential Issues

CALL OF THE HEADHUNTER

"**D**r. Smith, you have a call on line one."

"Who is it?"

"He said he's with Heidrick and Jackson."

A headhunter, you say to yourself. "Thanks. I'll take the call."

The headhunter's calling to ask, to urge, to beg you to apply for a presidency at A Fantastic College. Self-esteem, you have just been rebooted and upgraded with two zillion gigabytes of RAM! Talk about a great feeling!

But wait. Before you call a real estate agent and the mover, here's a warning and a little advice.

If you received a call about a job opening, especially at a good college, you can bet your next ten paychecks that at least ten other men and women heard the same pitch: "This job fits your skill set to a tee and they're looking for a leader just like you. In fact, (*your name here*), the job description for this position just about duplicates the great things you've done in your fabulous career. So, (*your name here*), when can they expect your application? Next week?"

Job hunting is exciting and, of course, a bit nerve-racking. So before you respond to the headhunter's call, don't take his plea too seriously. Headhunters routinely either understate or overstate the situation facing you if you do get the job. They will never tell you, "This is a crummy job that will break your heart." Instead, they'll say, "This is a challenging job that can be tamed by a top-notch pro like you!"

Do your homework. Take time to analyze as carefully and honestly as possible how your skills, interests, and needs match up with the job being offered and the challenges, resources, traditions, and expectations at the prospective institution. Also, it wouldn't hurt to get a second opinion from a trusted colleague—who knows the institution or may have some reliable inside information—to help clarify your thinking.

If you've applied, let your boss know or the board. We know a college CEO who attended a conference with one of his board members. They were mingling in the hallway when the executive director of the state faculty association walked up and congratulated the college CEO—with his trustee standing beside him—on being a finalist for a CEO job at another district. The faculty leader had no idea he was letting a secret out of the bag, a secret the president hadn't yet shared with his board.

MULTIPLE PATHS TO A PRESIDENCY

There are many paths that lead to applying for and becoming a college president, including recruitment by headhunters, public notifications of presidential job openings, as well as informal solicitation at conferences and off-campus meetings by faculty, administrators, and trustees seeking to build a pool of candidates for their college.

We know a multicollege district chancellor who sought a candidate for a presidential job at one of his campuses by recruiting a well-respected community college state association executive who had never worked a day on a college campus but who had demonstrated an ability to lead people and identify and articulate key policy issues.

The state association executive expressed interest in the job but asked, "Won't the faculty and administrators on the selection committee consider me a complete outsider?"

"Yes, they probably will," responded the chancellor. "But it's your job to show how you can help them be successful, regardless of your resume."

"And one more thing," the chancellor added. "I can get your name added to the preliminary interview list. But I can't get you a second interview. That's up to you."

FINDING A GOOD FIT

Okay, you've read this far and you're still interested in becoming a president or chancellor. Great, here are some things to think about.

It has been said that the best presidency you can get is one in which the previous officeholder had messed things up pretty well or was enormously disliked. Or as they put it in coaching, the best job is often with a team that just went 0-12.

But as we've tried to demonstrate in chapter 1, many factors go into deciding whether to become a CEO or president and which type of college or district you wish to lead. Do you prefer a single-college district to a multicollege district? And are you ready for the thrills and spills of a top job?

Family fit is also a big factor to consider. Children with special needs, family comfort with a rural versus urban district, distance from your spouses' family ties, and size of the "fish bowl" are all important considerations. Ask yourself, what sacrifices will your family be willing to make in terms of uprooting yourselves and all that entails? (These jobs are challenging enough without dealing with unhappy family members once you get on the job and face the challenges career changes invariably bring.)

The wrong job which is a bad fit can be a career breaker or, at best, slow down your progress. We know a colleague who thought he could, as they say, go home again. He had been a successful campus vice president and was ready to become a president in a multicollege district, which happened to be his home town, where he began his career as a community college administrator years before. But after getting the job, he discovered that the college had changed while he was away. The people had changed. The politics had changed. Even the academic priorities had changed.

The most relevant questions under those circumstances might be whether the campus still perceives you as you were when you left and whether they could accept you now in a much different role. You are not the same person you were back then and the college is certainly a different place. As the sixth-century BC Greek philosopher Heraclitus said, "One cannot step twice in the same river."

But once you've made up your mind which way you want to go, commit to doing the homework necessary to be a successful candidate. Here are some questions to ask the headhunter and colleagues in the field who know the situation at the prospective campus:

- Why did the previous president or CEO leave?
- What kind of board do they have?
- Are there likely to be any inside candidates?
- What stage in the life cycle of a college is the district in? Building? Maintaining? Transition? Repair?
- And what kind of president or chancellor do they need? Builder? Healer? Status quo? Change agent?

After you're satisfied with the answers, match your skill set against the needs of the district and make an honest assessment as to whether a good match exists. Don't put your line in every stream. If you're fishing for a halibut, you don't put your line in a trout hole. For administrators going after their first presidency or CEO job, remember: Many presidencies exist out there for you. Don't take just anything. There are positions out there that are career makers and career breakers. You don't want your first to be your last.

Be persistent. We know a president who served for many years as a chief business officer. To finally become a president, he had to overcome the well-known prejudice against financial officers when it comes to faculty and academic administrators sitting on presidential screening committees. But he did it by building a strong reputation as a statewide leader, not only among business officers but among all types of college leaders. He finished second place several times on CEO job searches before finally finding the right match.

YOUR FIRST CONTRACT

Several years ago a friend of ours was so excited about getting her first CEO job she almost let her enthusiasm get the best of her.

She was happily shaking hands with her new board when the board chair, in an altruistic act of unselfish friendship, offered the services of the college's attorney in drafting up the new CEO's employment contract. "Why don't we let old Fred write up the contract for us, Dr. CEO-elect. That way we keep it in the family and it won't cost you a penny."

Bad idea. At this point, big red flags should start waving frantically in your mind. In this case, the contract was negotiated and details worked out between the parties. A couple of days later, however, when the CEO-elect got home and received her copy of the contract to sign, she discovered, upon close examination, the contract was missing some key provisions that she had demanded.

Either the lawyer had made an innocent mistake or the lawyer and the board had unilaterally "renegotiated" the contract—and made alterations—after the CEO-elect had boarded the plane for home.

Get your own lawyer to either help negotiate the contract or at least review it carefully before agreeing verbally to its key elements and, certainly, before signing on the dotted line. Our experience has been that an attorney who helps you negotiate the contract can say things on your behalf that you might not be able to say without embarrassing yourself or getting the new relationship off on the wrong foot.

Your first contract represents your best opportunity to get a good contract that will benefit you throughout your career, whether you stay or move from job to job. Don't be greedy, but at the same time don't hesitate to establish the points important to protecting your interests and ensuring that you will be comfortable with the contract a year from now as well as five years from now.

Ask to see the previous CEO's contract, and try to get copies of contracts of other CEOs in the state. They both represent good starting points on which to build. Also, if in the hubbub of the selection process the board asks you to make a public statement before a contract is signed, simply say, "I'm looking forward to coming to XYZ College upon completion of successful contract negotiations." That puts as much pressure on the board as it does on you to come to a happy and swift resolution.

DEFINING THE BOARD–CEO WORKING RELATIONSHIP

Getting a good contract is critical. For you, your family, and for your employer.

But just as important is the CEO and board defining how they will work together. The first step: developing an understanding, or road map, of your role and the board's role in the emerging relationship between the district's citizen board and its professional management.

Some of the many issues that may be addressed: education and fiscal expectations for the college, evaluation process and timetable for the CEO, and who is responsible for hiring top staff, just to name a few.

Will your board, for example, allow you to select your own team? The point is important because it relates to accountability and your own survivability. As the new CEO, you need the authority to move your agenda, a task made a lot easier, and more fun, if you have a management team you've blessed—whether you reaffirm the folks that are already on board or bring in some new blood.

But, Dr. CEO, a board member might say to you: "The vice presidents often stay longer than you do. For our own protection, we find it imperative that we, the board, help decide who is put in those positions." And you should say right back to the board: "You're right. Selecting the best is important. And I'll make it my highest priority to find the best candidates to choose from. But if I'm going to lead, I have to have a team that follows my lead. You've hired me to get the job done. I can only truly be held accountable if I have a structure in place that makes that possible."

To work out that critical CEO–board working relationship, we know colleges that have brought in consultants to lead board retreats as part of the contract process. Their job? To help the CEO and board address a variety of issues, some seen as "territorial" or "turf" by both parties.

Not all district boards are going to go to this length to get ahead of the game, so to speak, but in many cases such an approach can led to fewer problems, fewer misunderstandings, and result in a solid working relationship right out of the gate.

ASSESSING THE BOARD

As you come to contractual terms on working with the board, a critical next step for the new CEO is to find out where the board is—in transition or steeped in the status quo? Is it a low-maintenance or a high-maintenance board? Do they need a healer or someone to challenge them? Do they understand that you work for the board, not the chair or an individual trustee?

Another critical first step is to determine how long a leash the board is willing to give you. Oftentimes this is defined by the degree of trust they have in you. Which may simply be a factor of how effective your first weeks and months on the job turn out to be.

Not too many years ago a college board we were quite familiar with hired a new chancellor to clean up a financial mess. Upon arriving on the scene the new CEO found that the faculty had successfully pushed the board to make faculty salaries among the highest in the state.

When the new chancellor identified the problem—pay raises that were beyond the college's financial capabilities—the board was *shocked, shocked* to hear the bad news. When the faculty, which had been active in raising campaign funds and walking precincts for incumbent board members, raised a ruckus over the new chancellor's conclusion, the board quickly reached its own conclusion. Obviously, the chancellor had erred.

Reading the board is critical for two reasons: (1) you want to keep your job and (2) you want to be effective in moving an agenda. To achieve both goals, you need to understand how trustees like to work. And you need to be able to assess the board's initial response to new program or policy proposals so you can package them in a manner that make trustees comfortable and supportive and in a way that allows you and the board to not lose face if problems do arise.

There are several steps you can take to help get an early feel for where the board stands:

- Read board minutes and talk to the previous CEO and district "historians" (such as veteran faculty members).

- Check the internet or even newspaper clippings to see which trustees like their names in the paper and the board issues that generate media coverage.
- Find out who's up for reelection in the next election cycle and if they are expected to run again or have political aspirations beyond the board of trustees.
- Pay attention to recurring themes in their questions, comments, and expressed opinions, as these can hold important clues about the values and issues of importance to your board members.
- Assess board member clout in the community and who in the community can influence their vote.
- Meet with each board member individually. Get to know their personal interests and background as well as their particular college-related interests, goals, and "hot buttons."
- Assess their tolerance for political "heat."

We know a board that included in its interviews with CEO candidates a unique approach to assessing the candidates' ability to grasp board politics. One of the trustees on this seven-member board would hold up four fingers and ask, "Do you know what this means?" The smart candidate would count the number of trustees around the table and figure out quickly that the board expected its new CEO to respect and respond to the board majority.

CARE AND FEEDING OF THE BOARD

Achieving success as a CEO is linked directly to the success of your board of trustees. As such, you must make board members look good as well as help them be effective.

It's important to learn about each member as an individual, including their professional, family, community, and political interests.

You'll find some board members high-maintenance and some low-maintenance. Some want to be taken out to breakfast or lunch every week; others just want the college to run smoothly with minimum conflict. In either case, it can be helpful—and make the job more pleasant—to discover the personal interests of your board members and to involve yourself to some degree in their outside interests. We've jogged on weekends with trustees, attended concerts with trustees and their spouses, and even gone to horse races and sat in bars. We've also attended a fair number of weddings, ball games, barbeques, and Fourth of July picnics with our trustees.

CEOs use a lot of different strategies to stay in touch with their boards between meetings. One we've found that works well is "The Week That Was" newsletter. We write it as if we're writing a personal letter, giving them not only facts but insights, trends, potential problems on the horizon, tidbits about staff activities, and our own comings and goings. It generates an intimacy that allows you to minimize the number of necessary one-on-one breakfasts or dinners. (When you like the trustee and his or her spouse, going out to dinner and having social contact is easy to do. But when the trustee is not your favorite person, that's when you have to grin and bear it.)

Care must be taken, however, to treat each board member with similar information and personal attention so they don't feel you have favorites. Some trustees will welcome the attention, some may not. But all have to be given the opportunity to receive equal attention from and access to the CEO.

A common impediment to good CEO–trustee relations is the trustee who becomes jealous of the CEO's high visibility in the community. This usually occurs when the trustee is not as well known or respected in the community as they would wish. We've known trustees suffering from this affliction to ask the CEO if they could see to it that they were also invited to the same parties and community functions as the CEO.

Be sure when the opportunities arise, such as a breaking ground ceremony for a new campus building or an athletic championship award ceremony or a major community activity, that you give the board front-row opportunities. You and your staff can hang back and let them shine! Presidents, vice presidents, and deans have many opportunities to be in the spotlight. Share it.

And be sure to send the board members all the same board material. Never try to second-guess whether one particular board member would find a piece of information you send to another trustee of interest or importance. Just send it, and let them separate the wheat from the chaff. You don't want trustees comparing notes and finding some are getting information others are not.

THE FIRST 100 DAYS ON THE JOB

People don't like to be managed, but they do like to be led.

—Robert Jensen

When a change occurs in an institution's leadership, everyone in the institution feels it. It ripples through the system and, like the start of a football game, can cause a positive buzz but also chaos and surprises.

Problems left unsettled or unspoken will inevitably arise. People will come to the new president to tell him or her their version of the college's past traditions and history, what major issues need to be addressed, how those issues should be handled, what the last president did right or wrong, and who the good and bad guys are. The new president will hear, "Before she left, President Jones promised me . . ." or the classic, "That's not how we did it when Dr. Jones was here."

As with a sports team, everyone is watching the coach to see what he or she will do, waiting to see who gets put into the game and who gets tossed out. The first impression you, as the new president or chancellor, leave during the first one hundred days may dictate how people perceive you for years to come. It's hard to turn missteps around or fix a bad first impression.

The first step for a new CEO is to assess the playing field. A good starting point will be the last accreditation report. Every frog has its unique warts and freckles, and a recent accreditation report can give you insights into challenges facing your institution, confirm your opinion, and give you guidance in dealing with potentially sticky issues.

If the stars are all in alignment, your college will just be starting the accreditation self-study, a useful process in helping you set your agenda and a valuable building block for strengthening your college's planning process.

Next, get yourself out of the office and onto the campus and into the community to meet people, establish relationships, and conduct intelligence gathering. We can't emphasize enough the value of the "touch and feel" approach to leading a community college. After all, the term *community college* means the college is part of the community.

Meet and interview key staff and faculty and find out how plugged in they are and which ones are opinion makers and will be helpful in your effort to move an agenda. Next, find out who the movers and shakers are in town and go out and introduce yourself and shake their hands and find out what makes them tick. It can be helpful to figure out how your institution is judged in the community and who in the community holds sway over your board members and whether your board members can actively help you in the community.

After you've completed your initial assessment, what you've learned will help determine your approach to your personal and professional priorities. Am I going to play this job for the short haul or the long haul? Am I going to be the change agent needed at this institution or am I going to run at a pace that will allow me to stay? Some of the challenges you uncovered in your preliminary intelligence gathering may be so wrenching that if you do decide to deal with them you know you'll be gone sooner than you may have wanted. "I thought I was going to be a caretaker" you may find yourself saying, "but it's obvious I'm going to have to be a change agent if I want to best serve the college."

The next step is to build a strategy and, like a coach, develop a game plan to get your college moving down the field. Here are the basic ingredients:

- Set your priorities.
- Now rewrite your priorities, being more realistic.
- Set some priorities that will give you some quick wins.
- Work on selling those priorities to the institution. Organizing a collaborative process that ends up endorsing the same basic priorities you envisioned is a sound strategy in this era of shared governance.
- Get your board and leadership team involved from the start.

Warning: look out for board members, administrators, or faculty who say, "We really like you . . . but don't mess with things." Translated this means: "Whatever problems you discover here are problems we are comfortable living with." How to respond? Figure out fairly quickly what those problems are and under which rock they've been buried. Then you can decide which rocks you want to turn over and in what order.

PICKING YOUR TEAM

I never hesitated to promote someone I didn't like. I looked for those scratchy, harsh, almost unpleasant guys who see and tell you about things as they really are.

—Tom Watson Jr., legendary former CEO of IBM

The first personnel-related step when assuming a new presidency or chancellorship is to try to make winners out of everyone you inherit. (You certainly won't be able to change—at least in the short term—the majority of the management team you inherit.)

Every employee you now have has his or her strengths and weaknesses. A good leader has the ability to teach and mentor the average performers, some of whom, if given a choice, you wouldn't have hired but who have competence and are reliable. Any CEO, including mediocre leaders, can fire people. Successful leaders develop the potential in all their people.

When you decide whom to keep and which positions need to be refilled, don't clone yourself. Don't surround yourself with people who think like you or have the same skills set. You need to have a sense of what your strengths and weaknesses are and the self-confidence to hire people who complement your inadequacies.

When reviewing resumes, the title dean of instruction tells you absolutely nothing. We've seen the title assigned to the number two person on campus and to an entry-level division dean at another. Forget the title. In the interview, say, "Show me your college's table of organization and where you sit. What level do you report to? Directly to the CEO or a VP or assistant chancellor?" That will be far more informative.

And if you're an instructional person, obviously you will need a good student personnel dean and business officer. But more than that, you'll also need to find out what the institution needs at this point in its evolution. If you come into an institution and you're a good maintenance person, but the institution needs a change agent, then you better surround yourself with a few change agents to help you.

BUILDING YOUR OWN FACULTY LEADERSHIP

The best faculty leaders and best administrators on your team share similarities. They're bright, principled, and have good communication and leadership skills.

Administrators should recognize and acknowledge that faculty leaders/opinion makers can contribute immensely to helping move an agenda.

The best faculty leaders are quick on the uptake and have a good sense of campus politics and are opinion makers respected by their colleagues. Get them involved in the decision-making process, because if they're any good they'll probably bring some worthwhile ideas to the table and serve as a counterweight to the hidebound types on many campus committees.

They can also articulate that vision with their colleagues—in terms faculty understand and can support.

We know a faculty leader who inevitably ended up tweaking our ideas, leaving us with about 80 percent of what we had started with. But it was the most salient 80 percent and we figured 80 percent of something good is a lot better than 100 percent of nothing. So we went along with him and gave him ownership of the project and, as a result, had a potent salesman inside the faculty tent.

Some presidents face problems in finding good faculty leaders because many don't have a clue as to who the real faculty leaders are. Some faculty leaders—opinion makers—are not always to be found in the traditional leadership roles with titles such as senate president or union president. Some stay on the sidelines or behind the scenes where they can be just as effective.

And if you're a chancellor in a multicollege district and your presidents don't know who those real faculty leaders are, you're really stuck. It could be someone who has never been an official faculty leader but who may be a bulldog on the issues and, like a good politician, is not afraid to go door-to-door pitching ideas to colleagues.

Get to know your faculty, build relationships, and uncover the bright, savvy, positive, charismatic instructors and encourage them to get involved. If they fit the above description, don't worry about whether they agree with you on all the issues. They won't. But if you can't sell the bright ones on your vision, then maybe your vision is out of focus.

LEAVING A LEGACY

The greatest legacy a CEO or president leaves won't be found in architectural drawings or square footage added to a campus but in the men and women the CEO or president hires, promotes, and mentors.

The faculty and administrators you bring on board during your tenure will probably teach and lead long after you've left. Their success or failure will be the real bricks and mortar of the college and your true legacy.

A good case can be made that faculty are more critical to the central core of the institution's success than administrators. Tenured faculty generally stay twenty or thirty years, contributing to the life of the institution and affecting thousands and thousands of students.

The most important thing we do at our institutions is to teach students. It makes sense, therefore, that the president of the institution should be intimately involved in the selection of the faculty and the building and fostering of a faculty that is as talented and dedicated as it is diverse, reflecting the racial, cultural, and sexual identity mix of the college and the larger community.

Historically, most institutions, because of a lack of turnover by faculty and staff and other reasons, face diversity challenges. As a result, we have a more diverse student body (as do most K–12 districts in your service area) than is often reflected on our faculty rolls. Time and resources should be dedicated, therefore, to supporting equity in personnel decisions.

But don't stop there. In addition, resources need to be committed to supporting diverse needs in the areas of mentoring and leadership training. And remember, it's not enough to promote a diverse classified, faculty, and administrative staff. We need to also provide a climate on campus where people feel comfortable and safe because, in some cases, some of these groups will be a small minority of the total staff.

CEOs and presidents may disagree, but we say that if you have to choose between spending time hiring faculty or administrators, we recommend you spend your time and energy selecting the faculty of the future. Obviously, the best practice is to find time to do both.

THE THEORY OF POLITICAL CAPITAL

A chancellor friend of ours was confronted with the startling realization that he had fired the wrong campus president. Here's what happened.

Not long after taking over the district, the new chancellor reached the conclusion that one of his four campus presidents was too slow getting on board with the program. No matter what approach the chancellor took to cajole the senior president, he refused to support the chancellor's new ideas. The chancellor subsequently proceeded to expend a great deal of political capital forcing the retirement of this respected but recalcitrant president.

A year later our friend came to the uncomfortable conclusion that the real impediment to success was not the president he had just dismissed but another president in this multicollege district. By then, other expenditures of his political capital had eaten away at his stack of chips and he was stuck with the real culprit.

Our theory of political capital in a community college may be described in terms of poker chips. Each new president, CEO, or chancellor arrives on his first day with a tall stack of chips. Beginning the second day on the job, that tall stack of chips begins to diminish, whether or not the CEO has spent any on his own accord. If he tries to remove deadwood administrators or reign in expenditures, the chips disappear at a faster pace. If he moves to alter the curriculum or improve faculty productivity, they disappear almost immediately.

The point? If you need to expend political capital to get something done, such as hiring or firing certain administrators, remember, the time you have the most chips to spend is early in your tenure.

One of your jobs is to decide which issues are worth expending those chips on and which ones aren't. Don't wait until that stack is just about gone to place a big bet.

And believe us, the chip bucket does not easily get replenished and certainly not on its own. You'll have to spend considerable time rebuilding your stack through effectiveness and success.

The worst case? Time—and chips—run out before that stack can be replenished.

IGNORANCE IS BLISS, SOMETIMES

An administrator friend of ours once served as chancellor of the same district, twice. During his first go-around, the district faced financial difficulties due to the fact that salaries and benefits in the district were the highest in the state. After he left, the board hired a chancellor to deal with the problem.

The new chancellor lifted the carpet, found the dirt, and, to her subsequent chagrin, refused to ignore it. The board, forced to examine the dirt by their new chancellor, gave a typical board response: "But this wasn't a problem when Fred was CEO."

"No," the new chancellor responded, "it was a problem, he just didn't tell you about it."

"But we liked Fred. Everyone liked Fred. And no one complained about the problem until you got here. Therefore, this must be a problem you created."

The faculty union, which played a major role in the election of board members, eventually helped run her out of office. Ironically, the former chancellor, who had been part of the original problem, got rehired to get the district "back on course."

Here's our rule: Once you know about problems on campus, you own them. If you don't know they're there, you don't own them. But once you lift up the rock and find the dirt, it's your mess. All rocks are not meant to be turned over! Turn over only so many at a time. And pick them carefully.

If you're a caretaker CEO this may be no problem. You can choose to keep the mess contained and out of sight and still sleep at night.

But if you're a change agent, you may not be able to walk by that rug without taking a peek and feel a need (or obligation) to do some housecleaning.

If the board doesn't know what problems exist or doesn't have a clear sense of what the institution needs, uncovering the dirt can pose a major challenge for a new CEO—because they often *do* shoot the messenger.

Sometimes this is an opportune time for you to bring in a consultant team to look at your priority rocks and detail the problems and offer possible solutions and then use that information to develop a strategy to address the issues.

Some of us can say to ourselves, "I want to be here ten years. I don't want to overwhelm the institution by addressing all the problems at once. I'll just look under one rock at a time." That's a good approach, especially for a CEO with a mortgage and three kids to put through college. But here's a better idea that gets the same result.

Look under all the rocks and then prioritize the problems you find underneath. Better that you know the whole picture, because how you deal with the first problem you choose to tackle will have an impact on how you eventually deal with the others.

TRUSTEE ELECTION POLITICS

A board of trustees at war with itself, its CEO, or the college is usually a board that could benefit from some new blood. In states where local citizens elect trustees, the possibility of removing problem trustees through the election process can be a delicious temptation for CEOs tired of unprofessional, destructive, and career-threatening behavior.

But sticking your neck out to support one candidate over another in a trustee election—especially if it involves backing a challenger against a sitting incumbent—can be perilous. Obviously, it's much easier for unions to back candidates. A winning trustee opposed by the union can't fire an entire faculty or support staff.

The best way to approach the task of exorcising an unwanted trustee through the election process is the route taken by the chancellor of a large multicollege district we worked with. He went to a friend who went to a friend who was a retired and highly respected former state legislator in the area. The pitch to the retired legislator from the friend of the chancellor went something like this: The incumbent trustee of the college district that serves the community you love has blocked the school's development. The incumbent is not in tune with the education goals of the community. He has become, in fact, an embarrassment to the community and the college district. You are the only possible candidate that can defeat him at the polls and, in turn, save the district.

The approach worked. Not only did the retired legislator run and win a seat on the college board, but no direct tie linking the chancellor to the winning trustee ever surfaced. The losing candidate and the other board members could only speculate why such a prominent community leader challenged the incumbent.

You don't want your fingerprints on trustee elections. If you lose, you're dead. And even if you win, you raise the question in the minds of the other trustees: "Well, if he did that to Jane, he may do it to me." Be sure someone else does the dirty work.

Unions are going to be involved in trustee elections in states where trustees are elected locally. Significant financial incentives exist for them backing one candidate or slate of candidates for a board seat. But unions don't always get away with it. It's a guilty pleasure for administrators to watch a union pour money and time into a candidate's successful race and then watch the newly elected trustee come on board and discover the truth about budgets, personnel practices, student-to-faculty ratios, state laws governing community colleges, and so on. Sometimes, as one union friend of ours said, "They don't always stay bought."

VOTES OF NO CONFIDENCE

The less there is to fight over, the bigger the fight.

—Pat Kirklin

In some states, votes of no confidence in the president or CEO have become so commonplace that a pretty good-sized room would have to be rented to hold a meeting of this not-so-exclusive fraternity.

The most common cause: faculty union dissatisfaction with its current contract or a lack of progress in collective bargaining negotiations. The second most common cause: faculty dissatisfaction with the style of the CEO or the direction the college is taking.

Faculty may view a vote of no confidence as a bargaining chip in pay and benefit negotiations or as a hammer to be used when disputes over major education, budget, and personnel issues reach an impasse.

A newspaper once quoted a faculty member commenting on a dispute between the instructional staff and the college president: "Our president hates faculty and his priority is not in the classroom." Translation: the union wants a raise. Another newspaper quoted a faculty union president regarding the board: "They are not the only taxpayers in this community concerned with educational excellence. There are nearly 1,000 such taxpayers who teach 25,000 students who, too, are concerned about accountability and economic efficiencies." Translation: the union wants a raise.

If the vote of no confidence stems from a labor dispute, the source is usually transparent to the board and the community and the no confidence vote usually can be survived by the CEO. In this case, the president should be sure to clarify the issues and keep the lines of communication open both on-campus and off-campus because sometimes the facts get confused and misinterpreted. This could include outreach to community opinion makers and the appropriate media.

However, if the faculty is unhappy with the working style or personality of the CEO or direction the college or district is taking, these are much harder for the CEO and the board to explain to the broader, noncollege community.

Depending on the degree of animosity, sometimes these issues can be mitigated through discussion or mediation between the players, sometimes with a third party getting involved. But if the issue or issues have persisted over time and the parties have solidified their positions and the situation cannot be remediated, the board and CEO need to confer on next steps.

Unfortunately, sometimes the next step is for the CEO and board to accept the reality of the situation and negotiate the best terms of separation.

CAN YOU HEAR THE POSSE COMING?

The survival rate for managers is much higher than it is for leaders.

—Robert Jensen

When is the best time to leave?

The message that you should leave can come in many forms. It might be the board's hesitancy to discuss a contract extension; a trustee's "kidding remark" that your career would flourish better somewhere else; or a subtle but detectable shift in attitude at public board meetings. Maybe your comments and opinions are not always sought—or welcomed. Or worse, the board no longer quickly jumps to your defense at board meetings but allows criticism from the audience to linger like pungent cigar smoke.

Another trigger may be the fact that you have applied for a job or two, didn't get them, and suddenly the board is saying to itself, "What don't we see in our president that others don't like or want?" or "Why are you so anxious to get out? Don't you love us anymore?"

So when is the best time to leave? Sometimes when it would not only be good for the district but be in your best interest as well. Frankly, sometimes you've done all you can do and to stay would mean the district will just glide. You may have pushed as hard and as far as the institution will allow.

On the other hand, one tried and true sign it's time to leave is when everybody's happy and there is no tension present on the campus. Happiness and a stress-free environment usually mean you're not stretching your people or yourself.

As a professional, you may just want some new scenery and are tired of dealing with the same players, the same challenges and feel you have given all you can give. There is nothing wrong, professionally or ethically, with leaving a job at the "apex" of the curve when things are going well and you're feeling good about your achievements and your contract.

We know CEOs who freshen up their resumes and begin to seek new pastures *after* their multiyear contracts have been extended one or two times.

CEOs who can stay longer than ten years have great staying power and are the special ones. But if people are clamoring for you to leave, it may not be your fault entirely. You may have made some tough decisions that needed to be made or the college may have just gotten tired of your bag of tricks and wants a new magician.

5

Not for Trustees Only

BECOMING A TRUSTEE

If we were asked to open a community college trustee Hall of Fame, we could easily pick a roomful of trustees who, as a result of their wisdom, vision, and dedication, have made their colleges a better place for students and a powerful force for good in their communities. If, on the other hand, we were asked to create a board Hall of Shame, unfortunately it would be easy to select a roomful of trustees who, as a result of their selfishness, bad judgment, and public spite, diminished their college in the eyes of students, employees, and the community.

Probably the most unsettling time possible for a college occurs when a new trustee or trustees take their seat at the board table. Typically, the concern is not over whether the trustee will demand the college improve or expand its services, but the types of personal or political issues the new trustee will want addressed.

If you are convinced you have the answers to improving faculty morale, or what software the college should purchase to run its fiscal operation, or who should get hired for this job or that, don't seek the board seat. Please.

And if your goal is to be a full-time politician and you see your election to the community college board catapulting you into the White House, run for the city council instead. Far more city council persons get elected to higher office than do community college trustees. Community college trusteeship is often incompatible with a political career since visibility, controversy, showmanship, and attention-getting activities run counter to responsible college stewardship.

Candidates for a trustee seat should give serious thought to why they want to be on a board. What is their motive? To be a good citizen? To make a difference? To run for another political office? To get something in return, such as college-paid health insurance, recognition, or respect?

If your answer to the question why you want to be on a community college board includes any of the following, you're probably not a good candidate:

- "I know what it takes to straighten that place out."
- "I just retired as an employee at the college and I know the real truth about what is wrong with the place and am eager to boss the president around."
- "I don't have a job, so I can spend lots of time on campus helping the faculty and staff."
- "I teach at a neighboring community college, so I *really* know the score."

If, on the other hand, you want to be part of a leadership team, a board, and a college focused solely on and dedicated to serving students, then great. Welcome aboard.

STARTING OFF ON THE RIGHT FOOT

New trustees are by their very definition new to the job. They are most likely either going to have some new ideas on how things should be done at board meetings or ideas on campus programs or services.

A guaranteed way for you as a new trustee to get a good, common-sense idea rejected would be to show up at your first board meeting and announce that you have completed a study that demonstrates beyond a shadow of a doubt that the college is not being managed properly.

We saw this done once by a new trustee who described himself during his inaugural meeting as the board's watchdog for the taxpayer. The other trustees winced at the not-too-subtle implication that they weren't watchdogs for the taxpayer and reacted to his subsequent recommendations with all the enthusiasm of a cat for a bubble bath.

Another brand-new trustee we know unveiled a chart at one of her first meetings showing the college had too many managers. She was genuinely puzzled in the weeks and months ahead by the CEO's hostility to her subsequent proposals and questions.

First impressions do count and set a tone for a trustee's success. Examples exist on nearly every college board of new trustees who alienate veteran trustees (often by implying greater wisdom or higher moral standards) and then become frustrated when even their good ideas are ignored or rejected. Nobody likes a know-it-all, especially one who's just arrived on the scene. Human nature tells us we often shun such interlopers, even to the point of rejecting ideas that would be embraced if submitted by team players.

Veteran board members need to remember that new board members are just that, new. Veteran trustees should do everything possible to make a new board member feel welcome. Resist saying, "We do it this way" or to correct them when a new trustee offers a new idea or makes a public statement that might not be 100 percent accurate. Show patience, don't be defensive, give them time to learn and to even skin their noses a few times. Embrace them and bring them into the fold and into the family. Build a relationship based on providing information about the culture of the board and respect for both the mission of the college and the new trustee.

Probably the best rule for new trustees goes something like this: sit, listen, and keep comments to a minimum. Even if you have a solid grasp of the issues, your goal should be to first build relationships and get a sense of how the board members work together. There will be plenty of time for making your views known. The first few months on the job should be spent plowing the ground so that when you do speak out, people will listen to you as a peer and a colleague and give your ideas a chance to take root.

RABBITS CARRYING THE LETTUCE

We once attended a board meeting where a purchasing issue arose. One of the trustees happened to be an employee of one of the vendors being considered. Instead of stepping away from the table and recusing herself from the discussion, the trustee questioned staff members at length about a competitor's product.

If you do get elected or appointed to a board, remember there is a good reason why rabbits are not trained to carry lettuce. *Webster*'s defines the word *trustee* as "occupying a position of trust." Trustees are empowered with significant fiduciary responsibilities, including those related to purchasing, personnel, and budgets. Board members who have direct or indirect conflicts of interest should not participate in discussions or decisions that raise questions of ethical propriety.

For example, board members who take campaign donations or receive endorsements from employee groups and then vote on employee pay raises walk a thin ethical line. The constituency of a board member is the community or state, not the employees of the college. Allow us to say that again, because having worked with board members for more than thirty years, we're convinced that many don't get it: *The constituency of a board member is the community, not the employees of the college.*

Far too often, trustees get on a board and, because they spend so much of their time looking at campus issues involving college employees, develop an affinity for employees and begin to believe that they are accountable to the employees. This approach to college stewardship completely inverts (and perverts) the oversight responsibilities of lay board members.

Here is another example. The faculty union at a college we're familiar with has been successful over the years pushing the faculty pay scale to the sky by getting trustees elected to the board who are willing to pay off political favors. The union, already perceived historically as confrontational and liberal, has, however, never allowed its politics to get in the way of its real goal, higher wages and better benefits.

That's not to say that people don't deserve to be paid fairly. But there has not always been a good balance between the care and feeding of people and the care and feeding of the educational program.

Some colleges have disassembled programs that directly affect students in the classroom in order to cover salary and benefit issues. However, in a situation where this approach seemed warranted, the long-term impact of going this direction eventually gutted the quality of the educational program and was neither financially or educationally sustainable.

> *A budget is more than just a series of numbers on a page; it is an embodiment of our values.*
>
> —Barack Obama

PICK UP THE PHONE

The simplest act of good trusteeship also suffers the most abuse. If a trustee truly wants a good response to a tough question at an upcoming board meeting, the best way to get that response is to call the CEO in advance of the meeting. In other words, there are no inappropriate questions, but there are inappropriate times to ask a question. No one wants to be surprised. A trustee or a CEO.

Effective board leadership and oversight begins with open and civil communication between trustees and the CEO. From good communication flows information, ideas, cooperation, trust, respect, consensus, and good decisions. If someone on campus or in the community brings a campus problem to you, don't try to solve it. And don't keep it a secret until the board meeting. Take it to your CEO immediately by telephone or in a private meeting. Don't blind-side him or her at a public board meeting with it.

For example, if you have a question about why a particular faculty member or administrator might get hired or if you have information that might be damaging or embarrassing to any prospective employee, call (don't email or text, you can't be sure the CEO will have read it) and let him or her explain or, if appropriate, withdraw the name until the problem can be checked out. Or if you receive new information about a faculty union or faculty senate issue coming before the board or receive a call from someone with an allegation of misbehavior, call the CEO and board chair before the board meeting and give him or her a heads up and a chance to respond or get a response.

A CEO who treats his or her board members openly and honestly should be able to expect reciprocity. Conversely, trustees should expect similar respect from the CEO and his or her staff. (*For more on this key aspect of the CEO/ board relationship, see "The Importance of Loyalty" in chapter 3.*)

PRESENTATIONS TO THE BOARD

Here are some benchmarks you can use to judge whether the CEO and his leadership team are doing a good job at public meetings:

- For board meeting presentations on the big issues, the CEO should always set the stage beforehand so there are no major surprises for trustees or members of the college community. For example, when awarding a major construction contract or consultant bid or collective bargaining agreement, the CEO should, in advance, alert the board and key college leaders to any possible political, education, or budget controversies that may arise. Again, this is part and parcel of our "no surprises" management rule.
- Board presentations should be kept crisp, between ten and fifteen minutes long. Administrators must resist the temptation to try to demonstrate the depth and breadth of their knowledge by forcing the board to listen to unnecessarily detailed descriptions. (If they want more, they will ask for more. Give them the time, not how you built the clock.)
- The presentation should focus on the big picture. That is, faculty and administrators should describe how their program or service fits within the mission and function of the institution.

SELECTING THE BOARD CHAIR

In 1970, the rock-funk band Sly and the Family Stone released a classic you can still hear on the radio, "Everybody Is a Star." The song includes the line *"Everybody wants to shine."*

When you work with a community college board, it's helpful to keep the song's words in mind. One way to make the dream of stardom come true for trustees is to rotate the board chairmanship every year. Most trustees want the chairmanship on their resume. And just about every trustee wants a turn to shine.

We know most CEOs disagree with this approach. They would rather have their best board member or their handpicked trustee serve as chair. But that sends a signal to the rest of the board that the chair is more important than the other trustees, and that message can end up dividing the board.

Several advantages emerge when rotating chairmanships. For one, we think it makes bad board members better. When every trustee knows it will sooner or later be his or her turn to wield that gavel and have his or her neck out on the public chopping block, trustees tend to behave the way they want their colleagues to behave when it is their turn in the chair. It also allows board members to gain new knowledge and obtain a different perspective on how the board agenda is developed and a better understanding of their CEO's thought processes, priorities, and professional pressures.

Also, going through the sometimes bruising board chair election process each year can turn good trustees against each other. Cliques begin to form and memories of past board chair elections can shade the debate and influence voting decisions. Trustees start voting on issues based on who supports whom for board chair rather than on what's good for students or the institution.

Also keep in mind that seating arrangements at a board meeting do make a difference. Who should sit at the board table? Faculty, students, vice presidents? Contrary to recent shared governance trends that encourage a Noah's Ark approach to seating arrangements, we believe the fewer the better. You don't see state or federal legislators inviting the public to join them at the table.

Boards invite confusion and misconception if they become too inclusive. Nontrustees, such as the president of the faculty union, might be led to conclude that if they sit at the board table and regularly participate in the board discussion, that must mean they are as informed (or more so) as trustees. And like board members, a faculty union leader has a constituency. Which in their minds may be just further justification that they deserve a vote.

Our advice: keep the board and CEO separated physically from the campus constituencies. It minimizes the confusion and clarifies and elevates the unique role the board plays on campus as the primary and ultimate stewards of public accountability in the district.

KEEPING A GOOD CEO

Search all the parks in all your cities. You'll find no statues of committees.

—David Ogilvy

We are all familiar with the complaints, warnings, scholarly papers, and handwringing over the issue of CEO turnover. Shared governance, tight dollars, and dysfunctional boards have been found guilty in the "literature" and at conference cocktail hours of driving the average CEO tenure down to five years for multicollege CEOs and a bit higher for single-college CEOs.

We believe that progress toward educational excellence is hindered by a merry-go-round of presidents. If you change CEOs repeatedly, you never give your college or district the chance to develop and stick with a long-term plan. Plus, your institution may get a reputation among community college leaders as a difficult place for administrators to be successful.

Having stability and continuity in the district greatly influences the college's internal climate, including the morale of faculty, classified staff, and the administrative team. If the CEO is moving the college's educational agenda forward, the board should do everything possible to keep that progress and success going. A board can be effective only if the CEO is effective. Keeping a good CEO is as important as finding a good one in the first place.

Here are five cost-free things you can do to keep your CEO happy:

1. Follow the "no surprises" rule: keep the CEO informed and ask your questions about agenda items prior to board meetings.
2. Make sure everyone on campus knows that once the board makes a decision and the CEO has been given directions, no trustee will act to undermine the CEO's efforts to carry out board policy.
3. Support the CEO, especially when he or she has been carrying out the will of the board.
4. Own decisions and actions you asked the CEO to implement by articulating publicly that it was board directed, especially when it will be or is unpopular.
5. If you hear about a problem on campus, don't try to solve it. Take it to the CEO for resolution.

And finally, once in a while, say, "Thank you, Dr. CEO," both privately and publicly. Good CEOs make the resolution of complex, difficult problems or disputes look easy. As a result, sometimes boards don't understand or aren't appreciative of the behind-the-scenes wrangling, time, and sweat put into resolving tough issues.

EVALUATING THE CEO

We were recently talking with a chancellor who has an interesting approach to CEO evaluation. Once a year, at the behest of the board, she sends out a six-page evaluation form to faculty, staff, administrators, and community members, asking their opinions on how the chancellor handles a multiplicity of tasks. This is what business calls a 360-degree evaluation.

We think that's a bad approach. CEO evaluations are important. Getting the opinions of the wide range of groups who work with the chancellor can provide valuable information. But selecting the right cohort of respondents and the unique questions asked of each group is also important.

For example, how can a community member respond to the question: "How does the president work with the faulty?" or "Evaluate the effectiveness of the CEO in meeting the goals the board has set for the institution?"

No doubt, customized questionnaires sent to people who have direct (or should have direct) interaction with the CEO can be helpful to the boards and the CEO.

Customized questionnaires may go out to faculty, classified and administrative leaders, and community leaders with direct knowledge of the campus environment, including foundation board members, advisory committees, and city, county, and area school district leaders.

Well-thought-out questions can give board members answers that really help them understand how their CEO is doing. For example, if the board insists the president increase the budget reserve to 5 percent, and as a result there were no pay raises for the year, the question to faculty and staff leaders might read, "The board demanded fiscal accountability this year. Comment on whether you believe the CEO responded to our directive in a manner that is appropriate to our community college." Another significant question would be, "How well has the CEO responded to the board's goals and objectives for the past year?"

Questions such as "Is the CEO effective in public meetings?" or "Does the CEO relate well to faculty?" may not be as important as the question of whether the CEO is moving the college forward as directed by the board.

Another issue of CEO evaluations is whether the CEO should provide the board with feedback on the CEO/board working relationship. If the board and CEO are operating as a team, both parties need to share how that relationship can work at maximum efficiency. Often board members don't know that there are a few things they could do—or stop doing—to improve the CEO–board effort. We think CEOs providing boards with feedback is a good idea, but it requires a mature, solid relationship.

CEO evaluation is also a board-ethics issue. If, for example, you ask the CEO to make faculty more productive, how do you expect the faculty to react when it's time to evaluate the CEO? You shouldn't be surprised if they're unhappy. The faculty naturally assume that it was the CEO's idea and blame him or her. The board's goals and objectives should be clearly stated and publicly acknowledged each year. Make it a key element of board leadership: the willingness to stand up and publicly state what you expect from your CEO and then stand behind the CEO when he or she carries out your orders.

SUGGESTED STEPS FOR DEVELOPING A CEO EVALUATION PROCESS

We suggest the first step in the evaluation process, if this hasn't already been done, is a board meeting with the CEO to establish an evaluation process, including frequency and timelines.

The CEO and board chair should then work together to reach agreement on a series of questions for both the board and the selected cohort of respondents. Each trustee completes their questionnaire and sends it back to the chair, who summarizes the responses of both the board and the cohort of respondents.

The board then holds a special closed session without the CEO to review the individual trustee responses and the cohort responses, which have been summarized by the chair.

The chair then revises the summary based on the board-only meeting and shares this summary with the CEO in a second closed board session.

When the full board meets with the CEO to review the chair's summary, it's important for the CEO to hear from trustees directly. Often, a single member or maybe two will have a very different opinion about the CEO's leadership and effectiveness in meeting the board's goals and expectations than the full board or the selected cohorts that responded.

We have seen the situation, for example, where a trustee will make a serious accusation against the CEO that has been festering with this one trustee for some time. The evaluation process gives the board chair the opportunity to say, for example, to her fellow trustee, "When you say he's a dishonest so-and-so, what don't we know that you know? Do you have some information the rest of us don't?"

The CEO evaluation gives everyone—the board and the CEO—the opportunity to get issues on the table and off their chests.

WHEN IT'S TIME TO MAKE A CHANGE

Presidential longevity does not always equal a successful tenure. CEOs or presidents who stay ten years or more may end up treading water; their programs may become stilted and their staff unchallenged. We may be accused of contradicting ourselves here, but we believe that CEO job stability occasionally becomes just as big a threat to institutional excellence as continual CEO turnover.

Trustees should be on the lookout for too much complacency, fatigue, and insularity if their CEO has been on the job ten years or more. Complacency and fatigue usually exist as partners in crime. People in any profession can experience burnout, and the president may simply run out of gas. If the CEO allows the campus to become insular, that is, allows the bureaucracy to become so powerful and dominant that new ideas and initiatives have no hope of succeeding, then the CEO should be replaced.

When the relationship between a CEO and a board has failed—for whatever reason—and a separation becomes inevitable, the best advice for the board is to avoid "messing up the nest." You'll need it nice and tidy to attract a quality list of candidates to be your next CEO. Remember, everyone is watching. What respected and smart vice president or current CEO at another institution would want to go to a college (yours) where the board publicly humiliates its top staff?

DO WE NEED AN INTERIM CEO?

Is your college in need of repair? Do you want a professional who can turn lemon into lemonade? Instead of making a general search and casting about for anybody interested in applying, we suggest you go out and get yourself a hired gun.

What's a hired gun? A former CEO who is tough, battle tested, and willing to take an interim contract to clean up a mess, take a few body blows, and then get out of town, letting the next permanent CEO build on the foundation left behind.

Under what circumstances do you hire an interim CEO?

When the incumbent CEO suddenly leaves without giving the board a "heads up" and enough time to develop a sensible selection process or when turning the reins over to a vice president for six to nine months just might not work. The college may be facing such a significant challenge—a budget or accreditation crisis immediately comes to mind—that a long, drawn-out search process would delay immediate, necessary action and a sitting vice president or vice chancellor may not have the experience and skills necessary to deal with this type of crisis.

Warning: If you appoint an internal candidate for the permanent job to serve temporarily as an interim, and they then apply and are ultimately selected as the next permanent CEO, they and the board run the risk of the appointment being tagged as a biased selection by both the campus and the unsuccessful candidates.

In short, signing up an outside hired gun as an interim CEO spares the board the time and expense of a general search and allows the board to pick an interim with the credentials needed to clean up a messy situation. In addition, this strategy can enhance the future success of your next CEO by allowing them to begin their presidency with a clean slate and without having to immediately address controversial issues.

The board should not only give the interim CEO an ironclad, short-term contract, but also make clear that he or she should expect to be strongly criticized for the tough decisions that subsequently need to be made. That's the kind of vision and courage often needed when a district has hit bottom or is headed in that direction.

A good interim should be able to quickly give you their best assessment of the issues they see the district or college currently facing and a list of priorities and necessary actions for addressing those challenges. Since the interim CEO is a short-termer, their honest assessment, without the veil of politics, offers the board a good opportunity to receive feedback on the challenge at hand and how best to act in the long-term interests of the institution.

Treat the outgoing CEO professionally and appropriately, which, in part, means in a manner that a potential candidate for the next job will understand and respect. Even if you are angry, the satisfaction of making your displeasure public won't be worth the damage you could do to the institution and its prospects for recruiting a top-notch replacement.

But what do you do when there are years left on your CEO's contract? If board consensus dictates that the district would be better served by a new CEO, one strategy might be to privately express to your CEO the board's intention not to extend the contract once it expires. "We're not going to buy you out," you say, "but it would be in your best interest, before our decision becomes public at renewal time, to move on. In the meantime, you'll have our blessings and best wishes in your job hunt. But remember, the clock is ticking."

Don't make your intention public or you'll end up with a lame duck CEO and, as a result, be forced to go to the expense of buying out a long-term contract. If the CEO doesn't get the message or pretends not to hear it, set a deadline, with the stated promise to go public with the board's decision not to extend the contract if the CEO isn't soon out on the job market.

Separations are inevitable in our business. How you handle them as a board will be critical to the college's image and reputation both as an educational institution and as a landing spot for your next CEO. As we said, you don't want to mess the nest to the detriment of your next CEO search.

WHEN A CEO BECOMES ILL OR INCAPABLE OF DOING THE JOB

Sometimes a CEO won't recognize a health problem that has affected his or her leadership or when it is time to leave or retire. We once knew a CEO who had served for almost twenty years in the top job, but because of age and illness was incapable of remembering the names of the very people he had worked with for many of those years.

When this happens, it is the responsibility of trustees to protect the CEO and his or her family and, at the same, safeguard the interests of the college, its students, and the school's mission. Trustees: be gentle, be understanding, be humane, but also take the appropriate action.

SELECTING A NEW CEO

The board's most important job and responsibility is hiring a new CEO. But boards often make several mistakes when searching for new leaders. Here are two big ones.

First, boards too often enter the selection process without knowing the college's needs. As a result, they may hire CEOs according to personal charm and/or professional style or sometimes a flashy résumé or an impressive job interview rather than the actual skill set needed to meet the college's needs in its current standing. This may lead to a bad fit.

The board must have a sense of the institutional issues facing the college and what skill set the next CEO needs to lead the college forward. Is the college in the building stage of its life cycle or does it need to heal itself from past problems? Does it need a change agent or a consolidator? One helpful source for determining your institution's situation is the last accreditation report. It should help you quickly assess the institution's needs.

Second, you've heard the saying "Boards tend to hire opposites." If a college has had a CEO with strong budget emphasis the past few years, the board may think they need a more academic-centered leader this time around. If they've been building a lot of buildings, they think the next CEO should be good at other elements of building the educational program. That's not necessarily the best way to approach the selection process.

Some boards hire a search consultant, who can help the college address some of these concerns. However, a search consultant does not guarantee the college a better pool of candidates or a selection process that runs smoother or a perfect match. An in-house process may work just as well.

In our opinion, there are four basic steps to selecting a new CEO:

1. Determine the college's needs in terms of its strengths and weaknesses and the leadership style needed in the college's next CEO.
2. And then, having affirmed the college's needs in terms of its strengths and weaknesses and the leadership style desired, the board should reach consensus on the qualifications it's looking for in a future CEO.
3. Next, develop a selection process that the majority of the board supports, including whether the college will use an outside consultant or whether the college will undertake an in-house search process.
4. Finally, the board needs to determine to what extent the selection process will involve the various campus employee and student groups as well as the larger community served by the college.

DOES YOUR DISTRICT NEED A SEARCH CONSULTANT?

We've seen successful searches with consultants and we've seen consultants contribute very little to a search.

If your district knows where it's going and what it needs from its next CEO and has a human resources office equipped to handle this task, you can probably run a successful search without the expense of hiring a consultant.

However, professional search consultants do, in many cases, lighten the burden for the district by providing direction and guidance in the search process, such as working with the selection committee and assuring that the board's priorities in the process stay on track.

A good search consultant who knows the community colleges has a broad network of contacts, knows a diverse collection of the young up-and-comers, and can identify for the search committee an appropriate number of strong candidates who appear to fit the needs of the institution as identified by the board.

Finally, at the appropriate time, ask your consultant to give you their professional insight about the finalists and how each of the candidates meet your college's specific needs. (*If your district elects to use a consultant, review section titled "Hiring and Managing a Consultant" in chapter 2 for more tips on getting the most out of an outside expert.*)

Whether or not your district uses a consultant or in-house resources, trustees should know neither path guarantees success. *The preparation work the board does in determining the college's needs in terms of issues and leadership style gives the district its best opportunity for a successful search.*

Don't be one of those boards whose members lean back in their overstuffed chairs and say, "Doggone it, we have a great institution. We pay a great salary. All we need to do is open the search and they'll come." We suggest the approach taken by big business. Help identify CEOs or vice presidents with the experience, skills, and vision that match the college's needs and get the consultant to make sure those people apply. Steal the best brains if you have to. (These are the candidates who probably aren't interested in moving, because they are happy and successful where they are.) The board has to be sure the search consultant, if one is used, brings a bunch of winners, not just a bunch of people looking to change jobs.

And don't expect that involving representatives of the campus community in the selection process will guarantee campus support for the new CEO. No matter how inclusive the selection process has been, if the new CEO is not getting the job done, the campus community will drop him or her like a hot potato, despite being inspected, approved, and given the good housekeeping seal of approval by every constituency group on campus.

RULE #1: STAY INVOLVED

Be sure your board is actively involved in managing the direction of the search process and the work of the consultant or lead staff person. Don't hand this responsibility over to a college committee. The presidents and chancellors are the only employees in the district you hire directly. Don't let that responsibility out of your grasp.

When you establish the selection process, be sure to give yourself the flexibility to consider all candidates you believe would best serve the needs of the college. Make it clear that the board reserves the right to add potential candidates to the list the screening committee will be interviewing. It's your process, your responsibility, and ultimately your decision. (*See "Multiple Paths to a Presidency" in chapter 4 for more on this issue.*)

Don't let a screening committee narrow the final group down to two or three finalists. Narrowing the field down too much gives the committee the power to, in effect, select the CEO by limiting the choice of personalities, skills, and experiences. We recommend the board receive six to eight finalists. (Invariably, one or more candidates will drop out or references won't check out.)

And don't allow the committee to rank the finalists. This is particularly dangerous. If you give a screening committee or a consultant that power and then don't select the number one choice, you could face a tremendous political battle and morale problem in the district. For example, if you select the candidate ranked number three, four, or five, she or he may become known as the "second best" or "third best," or worse.

Finally, if you can't agree on a candidate after the final interviews, work at it. Don't give up too easily. Selecting everyone's second choice is foolish, even if it means a quick end to your deliberations. In our experience, this has usually meant the district ends up with the second—or third—best candidate for the most important job on campus.

We don't believe you necessarily have to reach unanimous agreement behind closed doors on your next CEO. But it is important that when your selection is announced publicly that the vote be declared unanimous so the next CEO comes in with a clear board mandate.

The CEO's success is your success. Give both of you a chance to succeed for the good of the students and your community.

Ten Truths of Community College Leadership

1. **Every decision you make has three elements: educational, fiscal, and political.**

   Too often, we are good on the first and not on the other two. Too many administrators think, "I'm an educator, not a politician."

2. **No CEO ever got fired for having a lousy curriculum, but many have been fired for not balancing the books.**

   Seventy-five to 85 percent of our budgets are personnel. Budget is class schedule and student-to faculty ratio. That's why your vice president of instruction must also understand budgets. If you can't pay the bills, you're gone.

3. **Change is stressful and threatening—and will be resisted.**

   But occasionally, you as a leader must walk the path of most resistance and do what's right.

4. **Organizational conspirators are alive and well.**

   And some of them are wearing the same color jersey as you.

5. **Leadership and management are different skills.**

   We've never heard anyone say that Winston Churchill was a great manager.

6. Leaders must be self-strokers.

If you're looking for a lot of praise, you're in the wrong business. Besides, the people who come up and pat you on the back may be trying to stab you.

7. There are three sides to every coin.

The black and white decisions are easy. Our job as administrators and leaders is to clarify the ambiguity that dominates so many aspects of human behavior and our organizations. Leaders get hired and paid to make decisions found in the gray areas. If you can't deal with ambiguity, avoid or get out of the leadership business.

8. There are no secrets in a bureaucracy.

This is a hard one for most people to understand and accept. Always give your staff the full deck, fifty-two cards. Just don't tell them what trump is.

9. Not all rocks are meant to be turned over.

If you're the boss, every problem is your problem. But not all problems are meant to be tackled. Cut yourself some slack—let some of the small things slide. As a Zen master said, "The one who is good at shooting does not hit the center of the target."

10. Community college administration is a contact sport.

As a leader you should be trying to move an agenda and that means sticking your neck out; and when you stick your neck out, inevitably, someone is going to take a swing at it.

About the Authors

Robert Jensen, PhD, has been a nationally recognized community college leader since the 1970s, when he served as a vice president at Mt. Hood Community College in Oregon and then moved to California as the vice chancellor of the Los Rios Community College District (CCD) in Sacramento. He then became president of American River College, followed by years as chancellor of the Rancho Santiago CCD in Southern California and of the Contra Costa CCD in the Bay Area. His last campus position was as chancellor of the Pima County CCD in Tucson, Arizona. Dr. Jensen has served on the American Association of Community College Board of Directors, the American Council on International Intercultural Executive Board, and served as a leader for a wide variety of state community college boards, including the Arizona Community Colleges Presidents' Council and the California Community College CEO association. Jensen was one of twenty presidents to be asked to attend an AACC Presidents' Forum, has lectured at both the University of Texas and Claremont Graduate University and served on the board of the Western Association of Schools and Colleges Accrediting Commission for Community and Junior College. Dr. Jensen in recent years has served as an interim CEO at several community college districts and has been a consultant around the country in the areas of planning, institutional research, staff development, management, and collective bargaining.

Ray Giles had a forty-year career in community colleges as a public information officer, state association executive, and at the end of his career, managing director of a national community college consulting firm based in Sacramento, California. He worked at Merced College, Fresno City College, and the Los Rios Community College District in Sacramento as a public information officer. Giles then served as program director at the California Community College Trustees Association before taking an executive position at the Rancho Santiago Community College District (Orange County). For fifteen years he served the California Community College League, the statewide association of community college districts, as a vice president of programs and services. He and his wife, Kathy, live in Roseville, California. Both are graduates of Los Angeles Valley College. Giles also graduated from San Jose State University with a degree in journalism.

9 781475 873443